FLY RODDING ESTUARIES

FLY RODDING ESTUARIES

*How to Fish Salt Ponds, Coastal Rivers,
Tidal Creeks, and Backwaters*

Ed Mitchell

STACKPOLE
BOOKS

Published by
STACKPOLE BOOKS
5067 Ritter Road
Mechanicsburg, PA 17055
www.stackpolebooks.com

Printed in China

First edition

10 9 8 7 6 5 4 3 2 1

Cover photograph by the author

Cover design by Caroline Stover

Photographs and illustrations by the author unless otherwise credited

Library of Congress Cataloging-in-Publication Data

Mitchell, Ed, 1946–
    Fly rodding estuaries : how to fish salt ponds, coastal rivers, tidal creeks, and backwaters / Ed Mitchell.-- 1st ed.
        p.   cm.
    ISBN 0-8117-2807-2 (pbk.)
    1. Saltwater fly fishing—Atlantic Coast (U.S.)   I. Title.
SH464.A85M584   2003
799.1′6—dc21

                                                            2002155840

This book is dedicated to the organizations and individuals working to protect and enhance our estuaries.
Thank you, one and all.

Contents

Acknowledgments

Thank goodness there are people to lean on and learn from in life. Where would a writer be without them? A debt of gratitude goes out to my editor Judith Schnell at Stackpole Books. Thanks Judith for putting my words in print. And thank you Amy Dimeler and Trish Manney at Stackpole as well. A couple of magazine editors come to mind—Scott Leon and Art Scheck at *Fly Fishing in Salt Waters* and *Saltwater Fly Fishing*, respectively. Thanks guys. And a special tip of the hat is in order for Chuck and Janet Furimsky and Barry and Gerry Serviente over at *The Fly Fishing Shows*. Folks, I appreciate being a part of those events.

A long overdue thanks goes out to Ernie Beckwith, former head of marine fisheries for the state of Connecticut. Ernie, you not only do a fine job with our fisheries, you put up with my endless questions. The fly tiers whose work appears in this book deserve credit too. Thank you one and all, I respect what you do. Thank you Norm Cavallaro and Brian Owens at North Cove Outfitters in Old Saybrook, Connecticut. Thank you Phil Farnsworth, Capt. Joe Keegan, and Ken Lagerveld. And lastly, adieu Angus. I bet the good Lord has a salmon stream all picked out for you.

Introduction

We sat on the deck in the slanting rays of afternoon, making plans for a night of fishing. In the yard, trees swayed in a gusty breeze, the same wind that had carpeted the coast in whitecaps; clearly we had to look for protected waters. The salt pond down the road was high on our list. Not only was this small estuary sheltered, but it was also brimming with bait and striped bass. A check of the tide chart revealed that high tide would crest around 10 P.M., and we could expect an ebbing current an hour or so after. So we agreed to head over to the pond close to midnight.

Upon arrival, we put on waders and rigged rods and reels in the pale glow of a streetlight. Then we began the long trek in. The moon had been up since midday, but now its journey was nearly done. As it departed, the night grew increasingly dark. High above, the sky had been snapped clear by the brisk north winds, removing every veil from the heavens. And as we moved forward, freely the stars fired down.

Eventually we came to our chosen spot, a point of land where the ebbing current picked up speed on its journey to the inlet. For a moment we stood in silence, watching the dark waters. Writhing, murmuring in the starlight, the current was an immense black snake slithering to the sea. By now our eyes had adjusted to the low light, and our hearing too seemed to improve. Straining to pick up the least little sound, we listened for the muffled noise of feeding fish. Here and there, during a pause in the breeze, we could hear them. Stripers were nearby.

With growing anticipation, we waded in. Casting across the current, we worked to find the right range. As we did, occasionally a striped bass would lift from its nocturnal lair and latch on to the fly. The strikes always came as the line tightened below us, but somehow each strike was still a surprise. Instantly the fish was hooked. And just as quickly, it would turn to use the force of the moving water, peeling yards of line from the reel. Some of the stripers were small, and we could fight them by standing our ground. Others were far stronger. Coupling their strength with the power of the rip, these fish forced us to pull up stakes and follow along. Rods held high, we would move down the bank, dragged off into the night by a wild creature, while overhead, the Milky Way coursed the sky like a ragged river of stars.

Estuaries provide some of the finest fly fishing on earth. Not only do you have a variety of species to fish for, but these fish come in a wide range of sizes, from schoolies to memorable monsters. And you can hunt them in a variety of ways. You can do it under the sun or under the stars. You can probe deep channels with a sinking line or sight-fish in the shallows. You can work from a sandy beach or a grassy bank, or you can wade out on bars and flats. Or you can cover the water from a boat, and in many situations a canoe, kayak, or rowboat does just fine. Estuaries have a world of fishing to offer.

If you're a freshwater fly rodder trying your hand at the salt, you'll find estuaries particularly appealing. The heavy 9- and 10-weight rods used on the open coast are not mandatory here; 6-, 7-, and 8-weight rods, the ones freshwater anglers are accustomed to, are often just right. In addition, the scale of the terrain is more familiar. Estuaries don't have the endless horizons and menacing waves found on an ocean beach. Rather, these are smaller and more intimate waters. Here you can bite off a little at a time, until you have a feel for the place. Best of all, the angling education acquired on rivers and lakes can be applied here. Believe me, that alone is a huge help.

Estuaries are, by definition, any place where fresh and salt water merge. All told, they make up only one-half of 1 percent of this planet's total saltwater environment, yet their contribution to marine life is essential and far-reaching. Simply put, estuaries are both essential energy producers and energy exporters, natural power plants where the richness of the land is fueled back to the sea. That richness results in an abundance of plankton—the single-cell organisms that form the very foundation of the food chain. As a result of that abundance, healthy estuaries are biological hotbeds, nurseries, and feeding grounds for much of the marine life on the coast. As these species mature, they absorb the inherent richness of the estuaries, storing it in their growing bodies. Then, as adults, they migrate to open waters, living reservoirs carrying a precious cargo, ready to be consumed by the larger fish of the coastal world.

In terms of size and shape, estuaries are diverse. Some are little more than a trickle in the back of a quiet cove, known to only a handful of anglers. Others—such as Chesapeake Bay and Long Island Sound—are huge. In fact, each holds a lifetime of fishing for hundreds of thousands of anglers. Along with this diversity of dimension, estuaries also boast a diverse wealth of fish. Along the North Atlantic coast, they are home—in season—to striped bass, bluefish, weakfish, Atlantic bonito, little tunny (also known as false albacore), American shad, hickory shad, and fluke. Traveling southward to estuaries of the Mid- and South Atlantic coasts, you'll find many of these same species, but increasingly a new cast of characters begins to emerge. Now anglers find themselves casting flies to red drum, black drum, spotted seatrout, Spanish mackerel, small tarpon, ladyfish, snook, jack, pompano, and other species.

On the other side of the continent, estuaries hold just as much fly rod potential. In his informative book *The Estuary Flyfisher*, Steve Raymond reports that the estuary angler in the Pacific Northwest encounters surf perch, rockfish (not striped bass), starry flounder, ling cod, Dolly Varden, coho salmon, chum salmon, pink salmon, and steelhead. And there has long been a band of enthusiastic estuary anglers seeking sea-run cutthroat trout. These fine fish spawn in tidal creeks and streams and spend a fair amount of time in estuaries, providing dedicated anglers with a good deal of enjoyment.

Chances of catching a salmon on our Atlantic coast are, regrettably, slim to nonexistent, but several states offer opportunities for sea-run trout. In the Northeast, perhaps the best known sea-run fishery is the one at Connetquot River State Park on Long Island, New York. The trout here are rainbows, and the largest ever landed weighed a couple ounces under 20 pounds. New Hampshire's Berry Brook has a long-established sea-run fishery program, and Maine stocks fish into several rivers, including the Mousam and the Ogunquit. Connecticut started a sea-run program back in the early sixties with imported eggs from Sweden. It produced some monster fish, until problems with egg viability cropped up. Massachusetts once had a sea-run hatchery on Scorton Creek on Cape Cod. Both of these attempts were later halted, although residual populations exist.

In recent times, however, some northeastern states have shown renewed interest in sea-run trout. Connecticut has restarted its program, although it now uses Seeforellen brown trout for stocking purposes, since importing eggs is no longer possible. New Jersey got its program going in 1997, and as a result, the Manasquan River gave up an $8\frac{1}{2}$-pound brown in 2000. At the moment, these East Coast runs are small, but should they take hold, they promise to provide the estuary angler with an excellent challenge. And furthermore, these runs take place at a time of year when other angling opportunities are pretty much over.

Given all of the variety, this book can't cover everything that estuaries have to offer. The restrictions imposed by time and resources simply don't allow it. Instead, this book springs from the estuaries I have had the pleasure to see and fish. And though that is certainly a limitation, the pages ahead can still help anglers be successful in a diversity of locations. Whether the shoreline is home to palms or pines, throughout estuary fishing there seems to run a common thread: The way fish gravitate to current and structure, the way their hunting revolves around light and tide, and the way they react to wind and weather hold many similarities.

Before we head out on our journey, let me present a pressing concern. A few of our nation's estuaries are in pristine condition. Yet because estuaries sit at the junction of land and sea, the surrounding terrain is frequently highly developed and even heavily industrialized. This proximity to modern civilization means that estuaries are all too often degraded by a great many pollutants. When things are well out of hand, these pollutants may include heavy metals such as mercury, organic solvents, petroleum products, PCBs and other toxic chemicals, bacteria, and pathogens—all in all, an unholy brew. This destruction of essential habitat is—without a doubt—the largest single long-term threat to the future of marine fish. It's a bigger problem, and one that is harder to grapple with, than overfishing. So if estuaries get under your skin, please work to protect and preserve them.

CHAPTER ONE

Changing Conditions

Spend time on any shoreline and you're reminded that we live in a world of constant change. You'll witness the endless rhythm of the waves and the ebb and flow of light and tide. Perhaps you'll feel a shift in the wind, witness a school of baitfish swim by, or look up at the sky and see a turn in the weather. These things seem so elemental that we often take them for granted. Fish never do; for them, survival depends on their ability to adapt to nature's moods. And so it is— as every experienced angler knows—that the fishing can be dramatically different from hour to hour and day to day. It all depends on the conditions.

Given their proximity to land and their relatively shallow nature, estuaries experience a wide range of changing conditions—more so than open ocean waters. Estuary anglers must, therefore, be adaptable. With that in mind, let's look at the things you'll encounter and how to adjust your tactics and tackle. To aid in this discussion, I will mix in a dozen rules to fish by. These are general rules and not absolutes. Be ready for exceptions; you'll inevitably run into them.

To kick things off, I want to start by offering the two most important rules of all. *Rule One: Treat every day on the water like a treasure hunt.* Whether you're wading, walking on the beach, or riding in a boat, keep an open mind, be alert, be watchful. This is what it really takes to be a good angler, for fishing is, at its roots, a state of mind. Even when the fish have lockjaw, there is something to be discovered. Watch the water, the sky, the birds, the shoreline; what surrounds you is all interconnected. So make each outing a chance to learn more about your waters, to become closer to your surroundings.

Rule Two: Every fish you catch holds a lesson. Never forget this simple fact. After you release a fish, stop for a second and think about where that fish was

1

holding, the fly it hit, the stage of the tide, and so on. There is something to be learned from the experience. Granted, over time these lessons tend to repeat, especially when you fish the same piece of water again and again. But don't let that lull you into thinking that you know all there is to know. The next fish you catch may have a new story to tell.

WATER TEMPERATURE

With few exceptions, fish are cold-blooded. No wonder water temperature plays a profound role in their lives, dictating where they can go, when they can go there, and how active they will be. Every species has, for example, a temperature range outside of which it can't successfully survive. This range is often referred to as the species' thermal niche. Inside that range, there is a much smaller band of temperatures in which the species is very active and most likely to come to a fly—the fish's preferred comfort range. In estuaries, the waters are subject to swings in temperature, so the fishing is often highly seasonal in nature. The fish come and the fish go. And even where a particular game fish is a year-round resident, the fishing for that species is rarely good year-round. During some months, the fish are responsive to a fly, but during other months, they are more or less dormant.

Here's a look at the preferred comfort range for many of the popular estuarine species of game fish. For striped bass, the range is roughly 52 to 68 degrees F. Bluefish like it a bit warmer, 55 to 80. Red drum are similar, at 55 to 85. For Atlantic bonito and spotted seatrout, it's 65 to 75. Little tunny and Spanish mackerel like it hot too, preferring 65 degrees or higher. Weakfish are most active between 55 and 68, and so are hickory shad. I'm not sure what sea-run trout prefer out in the ocean, but they seem to run into estuaries when the water is pretty cold, often on the order of 45 degrees or less. These are preferred comfort ranges, not the only temperatures at which you can catch these fish. Striped bass can be caught, for example, in water down to 45 degrees or so. And I have caught bluefish and Atlantic bonito at 50. Still, the farther the water temperature is from a species' comfort range, the more you can expect that species to be hard to find and hard to hook.

When water temperatures are at the margin of a species' comfort range, those fish have to adjust, and so do you. Whether temperatures are borderline too cold or borderline too warm, focus your fishing on the deeper locations. Here the water temperature is apt to be more to the species' liking. Tide and time of day have an effect as well. For instance, in the heat of summer, the water near shore may be too hot for good fishing. But an incoming tide will bring cooler water to the shallows and greatly improve the angling. Likewise, those same shallows are going to be cooler during the low-light portions of the day. So even if the fishing is poor at noon, it may be fairly good at dusk and dawn.

Shallow water cools off and warms up more quickly than deeper water. Because of this, fish may migrate from shallow to deep and back again in order to seek optimum conditions. During the warmth of spring, game fish often move from deep locations to shallow ones in order to benefit from the warmer water found there. Conversely, on cold fall days, those same fish may drop out of the shallows to deep water where warmer temperatures prevail.

TIDES AND CURRENTS

Even when the water temperatures are in the comfort range for the species you seek, it doesn't mean fish will be everywhere in the estuary. Nor does it mean that fish will greedily whack a fly at any time of day. Far from it. Game fish regularly restrict their active feeding to advantageous times and places; this is a critical part of the survival game. And often they pick those times and places based on two factors: the stage of the tide and the presence of current.

The tide plays a pivotal role in saltwater fishing. It does so in several ways, but perhaps the most significant is this: Tides influence the movement of baitfish, and where the bait goes, so go the game fish. The tide accomplishes this magic by moving and concentrating plankton—the stuff that many baitfish feed upon. Plankton is, for the most part, very small and hard to see with the naked eye. Yet what plankton lacks in size, it makes up for in quantity. Truth is, plankton constitutes the overwhelming bulk of life in the sea, and it is exceedingly abundant in estuaries. And that is why estuaries can support enormous schools of baitfish. Plankton is largely at the mercy of the tide and current. A rising tide pushes plankton closer to shore and farther up inside an estuary. On an ebbing tide, the reverse happens: Plankton is pulled toward the lower end of an estuary and away from shore. Because plankton is what baitfish depend on, baitfish tend to move with the tide. So you can expect schools of bait, followed by the game fish, to swim up inside an estuary on the flooding tide and ride back down on the ebb. That explains *Rule Three: On an incoming tide, the angling action often moves farther up inside an estuary; during the ebb, the action moves back down closer to the estuary's mouth.*

Rule Four: Regardless of the tide's direction, focus your fishing where there is current. Tidal currents are responsible for moving the plankton, but they do something

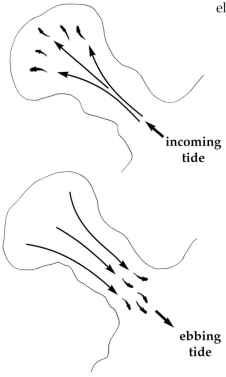

incoming
tide

ebbing
tide

*On a rising tide, fish tend to move far-
ther up inside an estuary, and then on
the ebb, they often drop back.*

else too: Currents funnel and thereby concentrate the plankton. And because the plankton
is concentrated in the lanes of current, that is
where the baitfish concentrate too.

Clearly, if you're going to plan your
angling adventures with tide and current
in mind, you must understand the tides
and currents in the area where you plan
to fish. Some of this information can be
obtained from tide charts or software, or
by getting advice from local experts. Still,
some of your education must come from
personal observation. Nowhere are tides
and currents more complex than in estuaries and backwater locations. Tide tables
are widely available for open stretches of
coastline, but finding a detailed tide chart
that covers smaller bodies of water may
be far more difficult. In some cases, they
simply don't exist.

Learning about tides and currents is
not difficult. Here are some basics. The
moon's gravitational pull causes the
ocean's level to rise and fall; hence the
moon is the master of the tides. This rise
and fall are what we know as high and low tide. During the new and full moon
phases, the moon gets assistance from the sun, and the ocean rises and falls to a
greater degree. These are called moon tides. The weaker tides during the first
and third quarters are referred to as neap tides.

*Rule Five: The greater the tidal range, the more powerful the currents, and the farther
fish travel with the stages of the tide.* The extent to which the ocean's level rises and
falls in a given location is known as the tidal range; this is usually clearly mentioned on any tide chart. Some sections of the coast have huge tidal ranges, on the
order of 10 feet or considerably more, while on other parts of the coast, the tidal
range is minuscule by comparison, barely 2 feet. Obviously the experience of fishing in an area where the water level fluctuates 10 feet is quite different from that
of fishing an area where the tide rises and falls only 2. Large fluctuations in water
level and strong currents also pose safety issues for boaters and wading anglers.

Thus failing to understand the tidal range not only will cut deeply into your angling success but may put you at risk as well. Know your local waters.

The published tidal range for any area is the average rise and fall; it does not take into account the larger tides associated with the new and full moons. At those times, the tidal range is often significantly greater, upward of 40 percent or so in some cases. This increase in water depth permits game fish to spread out to a greater degree in their hunt for food, reaching areas that might normally be too shallow for them to enter. This may also make them harder to find than usual, especially in broad, shallow bays and lagoons. Conversely, the ebb tides during these moons pull tremendous amounts of water out of shallow locations and thereby force the fish into increasingly smaller areas. This may make fish easier to find than usual.

In a few places, wind may be more important than tide in determining water levels. Here is a hypothetical situation. Some estuaries are very shallow bodies of water, with tidal ranges less than 3 feet. Imagine that your navigation chart indicates that at mean low tide you can expect 2 feet of water in the north corner of a large lagoon, enough to navigate with a shallow draft boat. But on a day when the wind is strong from the north, at low tide there may be only 6

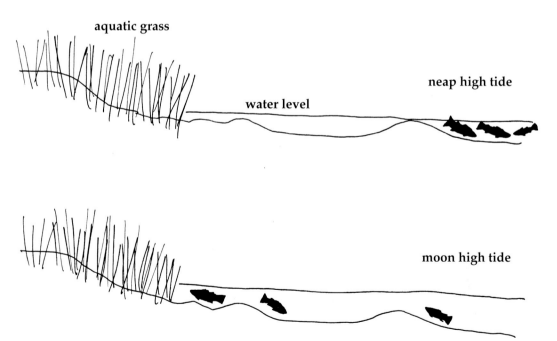

Expect fish to spread out more during the greater tidal ranges associated with moon high tides.

inches of water back there. Similarly, down at the south end of the lagoon, where the chart tells you there is 3 feet of water at low tide, there may be 5 feet or more under that same wind.

Beyond tidal range, you must also learn the schedule of the tides in your area. The times of high and low tides published on the local tide chart are typically for one specific spot, and that spot only. The time of tide for a place only a mile away from the one mentioned on the chart could differ by an hour or more. For that reason, it pays to obtain a tidal chart with information for as many different places in your area as possible. Acquire an up-to-date tide chart; last year's chart will do you absolutely no good.

In most locations along the Atlantic, a high tide follows a low tide every six hours and twelve minutes. Or think of it this way: There are two high tides and two low tides in just over twenty-four hours. These are called semidiurnal tides. Other coastlines may have a quite different tide schedule, however. For instance, the Alaska coast, the Gulf of Mexico, and the coastline of the China Sea have diurnal tides: one high and one low tide a day. Our clocks are set to a twenty-four-hour day, but it takes the moon twenty-four hours and fifty minutes to completely circle the earth. As a result, with rare exceptions, the time of tide advances each day. In areas with semidiurnal tides, it moves ahead roughly an hour.

Linking Moon Phase and Time of Tide

Since the beginning of time, moon and tide have moved hand in hand. And because of this, you can look at the moon and know the time of tide. Here's how to do it. In a given spot, the time of high tide on the day of the new moon is about the same as on the day of the full moon. Furthermore, the time of high tide on both moons remains unaltered throughout the year, although you'll need to adjust for daylight saving time. Likewise, the times of high tide on the first and third quarter of the moon remain fixed in a given location year-round as well. Once you're in tune with this celestial connection, a glance at the moon tells you the time of the tide.

Throughout this education, you also need to focus on how fish react locally to tidal changes. In addition to the fact that as the tide rises, game fish typically tend to move up inside an estuary, there is another general trend as well.

Rule Six: As the water rises, game fish typically move from deep locations such as channels to shallow structures such as flats and bars. Conversely, as the tide ebbs, fish typically exit shallow areas and move back toward deeper structures such as channel edges and holes. Here are a couple of examples. If you were fishing for redfish in the extensive salt marshes of the South Atlantic coast, look for the fish up in the flooded *Spartina* grass during the highest stages of the tide. Then, as the water recedes, those reds will exit back out of the grass and congregate in the adjacent waters, often picking deeper holes near points and oyster bars. If you were fishing for stripers in a Massachusetts salt pond, expect them to move to the shallows at the rear of the pond as the tide rises, and drop back toward the inlet during the ebb, often holing up along the deep edges of the channel.

Rule Seven: When game fish relocate—whether from shallow to deep water or from the mouth of an estuary to places up inside—they like to use the same route again and again. These preferred paths or travel lanes are typically associated with deeper sections of bottom structure such as channels, valleys, and trenches. If you know where these preferred paths are located, you can intercept fish as they relocate. This is a very effective tactic, especially in the larger estuaries, and particularly on flats.

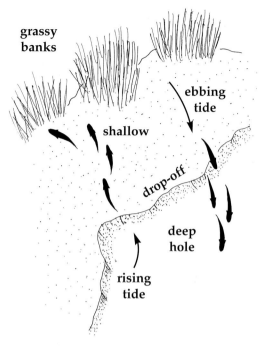

Along shallow shorelines, the fish typically move closer to shore as the tide rises and then drop back to deeper locations on the ebb.

Slowly but surely, you can apply your growing knowledge to specific pieces of structure, be they bars, holes, or flats. In that process, you may discover that some hold action on both the incoming and outgoing tides. It is far more typical, however, for a specific structure to be consistently productive on only one direction of the tide. The only way to discover which direction is best is to fish the place often; let experience be your guide.

Time of Current

Current strength has a significant role in where fish congregate. In the majority of situations, fish feed most actively in a particular spot when the currents are strongest. After all, that's when the plankton is most concentrated too. Typically, that translates into the middle hours of the tide. So the second, third, and fourth hours of the flood or the ebb are frequently prime times to wet a fly. But calculating when the tidal current should run can be trickier than you might think.

It would seem intuitive that the ebbing current should start shortly after the time of high tide. This is not always true, however. Very often in an estuary, the time of current lags well behind the time of tide. So, for example, the ebbing current may begin two or more hours after the scheduled high tide has crested. Likewise, the flooding current may begin two or more hours after the time of low tide. The amount of delay varies from estuary to estuary and is to a degree controlled by the size of the inlet and the area. On stronger tides around the new and full moon, the delay is apt to increase noticeably.

LIGHT LEVEL

Rule Eight: When planning your time on the water, consider light level in addition to tide. The feeding behavior of game fish is influenced not only by the rise and fall of the tides, but also by the rise and fall of the light level. Experienced estuary anglers are keenly aware of this, and they know that the finest fishing in a given location often takes place when a particular stage of the tide or current occurs at a particular time of day. With that in mind, they study their tidal charts for days to determine when the right combination of light and tide will take place and then plan their fishing expeditions accordingly.

If sight fishing is on your menu, naturally you need to plan your outings around the hours when there is adequate daylight. Typically, during the first few hours after sunrise and the last few hours of the day, there is not enough illumination to see fish on the flats. The strongest light occurs when the sun is directly overhead. Though this can be a good time of day for sight fishing, I find that when the sun is high but still angled—say from roughly 9:30 to 11 A.M. or 1:30 to 3:30 P.M.—the visibility is often best. The slanted rays create more contrast and make it easier to spot fish.

Say, for instance, that your favorite sight-fishing flat is most productive during the first hours of the flooding tide. You would then select days when that stage of the tide arrives sometime after 9:30 A.M. but no later than around 1 P.M. Since the tide advances an hour a day, you should find that there is about a three-day window of opportunity. Furthermore, this window will happen again in about two weeks' time, which means that this combination of light and tide happens twice a month, for a total of six days' fishing. Not bad.

If sight fishing is not on the agenda, your plans would likely be quite different. Frequently the hours of low light—from dusk to dawn—hold the most consistent fishing, particularly for anglers working from shore. This general rule

The rise and fall of the light can be as important to fishing as the rise and fall of the tide.

holds especially true during the warmest months of the year but is less the case in spring and fall. Suppose that you know a point of land where a nice rip current forms shortly after high tide. You also know that sunrise is at 5 A.M. You might then search the tidal chart for a day when high tide occurs around 2 A.M. If you get there around 3 A.M., the tide should be ebbing, and the strongest currents will take place just prior to first light. Nice.

TIDE LINES

In an estuary, fresh and salt water sometimes meet head-on. And when that happens, these two opposing forces may, for a moment, form a line. You'll often encounter this, for example, in the lower end of a river during the early hours of an incoming tide. If you study the water, you're apt to find a place where the force of the incoming tide is temporarily stalled by the pressure of the outgoing water. The intersection of these opposing forces is called a tide line.

A tide line typically shows up as a line of foam and floating debris. If the fresh or brackish water is discolored, the tide line is marked by a color change as well. These lines vary in shape and size. Some run fairly straight; others are as curved as a traveling snake. Some are barely a hundred feet long; others run

The vertical band in the right third of the image is a tide line. These areas may hold good fishing.

upward of a quarter mile or more. Regardless of shape and size, tide lines are worth investigating and may save the day when the action has been slow elsewhere. Nutrients and plankton are concentrated at these lines, and as a result, schools of predator and prey hang out here.

FORAGE

Rule Nine: Game fish follow forage wherever water temperature and water depth allow. Game fish are opportunists; they chow on a lot of things. Still, the bulk of their diet is usually composed of baitfish, and when and where baitfish are abundant, game fish are likely to be found. The reverse is true too: If there is little bait around, game fish are often hard to come by.

Estuaries are baitfish factories, and because of this, they regularly attract plenty of game fish. But even in estuaries, baitfish populations rise and fall from month to month and year to year. And the fishing fluctuates with those changing conditions. So it is essential that you understand what types of baitfish are found locally, which ones predominate, and where those baits tend to congregate. Furthermore you must understand the effect that season has: When do the baitfish appear? When do they go? You also need to know the size, shape, and coloration of these baitfish so you can match them with appropriate flies.

In the Northeast, several types of baitfish dominate the estuarine food chain. They are the Atlantic silversides, bay anchovy, menhaden, mullet, mummichog, river herring, sea herring, and sand eel. In all cases, these baits are present—at one time or another—in either adult or juvenile stages or both. With the exception of mummichogs, all these baitfish migrate with the seasons. River herring—alewives and bluebacks collectively—are some of the first forage of the year, entering coastal rivers as early as March. By April and May, some adult menhaden are moving in. By late May and early June, sand eels and silversides have arrived inshore for the summer. This is about the time juvenile sea herring are schooling up to leave salt ponds for the open ocean.

Come autumn, estuaries experience a massive exodus. Nearly all the baitfish must travel either offshore or southward along the coast to avoid the onset of cold weather. Game fish have been shadowing the bait all season and are ready for this event as well. As a consequence, the autumn migration of bait sparks perhaps the finest fishing of the year. The wise angler is well informed on the timing of these migrations. In the Northeast, the exodus typically kicks off as bay anchovies push out the inlets in early September. Look for sand eels and silver-

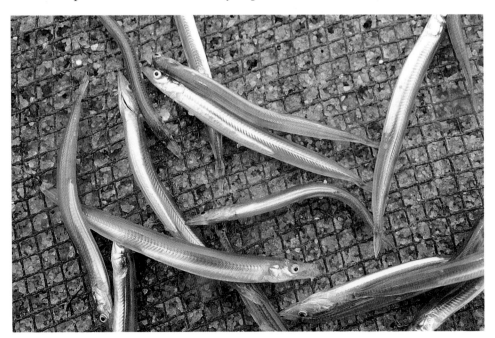

Sand eels are important forage items in much of the Atlantic.

Birds can often lead you to feeding fish.

sides to hold off until the first heavy frost of October. Menhaden are extremely hardy and will stay into November and perhaps even December in some years.

Rule Ten: When you're on the water, constantly scan the surface for signs of feeding fish. Given the critical link between predator and prey, it is imperative to keep a sharp eye out for signs of bait, and above all, for bait being attacked. Watch the water like a hawk. If you're observant, you'll catch more fish. After all, the single biggest issue we face is finding the fish. It's a simple reality that goes to the very core of all successful saltwater fly fishing. And sometimes it's simply a matter of opening your eyes. Diving birds, jumping fish, swirls, bait spraying across the surface, and slicks are common clues. When you see one or more of these things, where to cast is obvious.

Unmolested schools of baitfish are not that difficult to spot. Here again, birds can be helpful. Gulls have a habit of sitting on the water directly over schools of bait. If the bait is near the shoreline, the gulls may sit along the beach. Birds aren't the only way to locate bait. Patches of nervous-looking water or dark clouds in the water may indicate schools of bait moving near the surface. Plankton-feeding baitfish, such as menhaden, often come to the surface to feed, and the disturbance they make can be seen for a considerable distance. Look for dimpling of the surface, splashing water, and flashes of silver. Also look for baitfish lying on the beach. These fish have been driven out of the water by predators.

WATER CLARITY

Predator fish are mainly sight feeders, so water clarity has an impact on how easily they can find their prey. In addition, some species seem more sensitive to water clarity than others. Striped bass, hickory shad, red drum, spotted seatrout, and weakfish feed in even the muddiest-looking conditions. Bluefish are less likely to do that. Atlantic bonito and little tunny, in my experience, are clear-water fanatics and will quickly vacate areas when water clarity drops.

Even when fish are present, dark water makes it more difficult for them to find your fly. To counteract that, you need to make some adjustments. In clear water, fish can spot a fly even if it is running a fair distance overhead. In stained water, that is not the case. Because of the reduced visibility, you must deliver the fly to the fish's depth, and short of using a fish finder, the only way to do it is by varying the depth of your retrieve until you make contact.

Brightly colored flies help. Chartreuse typically shows up very well in turbid conditions, as do fluorescent flies in yellow, red, or orange. Big flies are easier for fish to find than small ones. It also pays to slow down your retrieve. And it may be best to fish during the brightest part of the day. Cover areas slowly and methodically; give the fish every chance to find the fly.

The water clarity of estuaries is typically lower than on the open coast. The extent to which it is lower depends on the exact location. Estuaries with sand

This water is exceedingly clear, but clarity can vary greatly in estuaries.

bottoms and little entering fresh water, such as the flats of Monomoy on Cape Cod, may be crystal clear much of the time. Locations with mud bottoms and those with a considerable volume of fresh water, such as the lower Connecticut River, may often be discolored.

All locations experience periodic changes in water clarity. Some are seasonal in nature. During the sunny months, plankton blooms often reduce transparency, particularly in estuaries rich in nutrients. In the salt marshes of South Carolina, water clarity is greatly affected by the passing of the seasons. During the cooler months from November to March, the water is at its most transparent, increasing your odds at the sight-fishing game. But from spring through summer, plankton blooms turn the water into a clouded broth, making sight-fishing nearly impossible. Up north in New England, plankton blooms also take place, but a bigger seasonal clarity issue is snowmelt runoff, which may discolor rivers.

Other changes in clarity are more temporal. One day the water may be gin clear; the next day it's clouded up; the following day the visibility drops to zero. It happens. These short-term changes are frequently the result of weather: strong winds, coastal storms, or heavy rain. Of these factors, wind is the most common. Calm conditions promote clarity, whereas wind produces waves, which stir up the bottom, especially in shallow bodies of water. The worst-case scenario is a shallow location with a soft mud bottom. The mud quickly goes into suspension, giving the water a smoky look, and in a matter of hours, water clarity takes a steep nosedive.

Flies in fluorescent yellow, red, or chartreuse are useful in turbid waters.

The stronger the wind and the longer it blows, the greater the problem. Wind direction plays a role too. Some bodies of water are long and narrow. A wind traveling lengthwise through these locations causes far more wave action than a wind of similar strength blowing across them. A north or south wind quickly kicks things up in New Jersey's Barnegat Bay, and the same goes for Florida's Indian River Lagoon. In Long Island Sound, however, it's an east or west wind that's most likely to get the whitecaps rolling.

Tides are another factor. After the wind stops, the flushing action of the tide tends to remove the silted water, restoring clarity to normal. In some locations, tides play a role in water clarity even when the wind is calm. During the ebb, the tide may suck murky water out of salt marshes and tidal creeks in the back end of a bay. Gradually this filters out over a large area and reduces clarity, particularly during the final hours of the tide. When the tide floods, on the other hand, it forces clean seawater back into the bay, clearing the turbidity. This effect of the tide is usually fairly subtle, but it can be significant to anglers who wish to sight-fish.

The effects of strong moon tides may be a mixed bag. On the flood, they can help clear the lower end of a muddy river. But on the ebb, conditions may deteriorate. These strong flood tides rise higher up into the intertidal zone and often sweep away large amounts of debris sitting on the beach. When the tide ebbs, it carries the debris with it, and water clarity can drop suddenly. Boaters should keep an eye out at such times for floating objects that might present a hazard. The powerful currents associated with these tides also stir up the bottom, placing silt into suspension. This is particularly a problem in areas with muddy bottoms. Consequently, the weaker tides around the quarter moons—what are called neap tides—often host the best visibility.

SALINITY

Salt water is just that: water mixed with salt. Over 80 percent of the salt is common salt—sodium chloride. The rest is made up of other minerals such as magnesium, calcium, potassium, phosphorus, and silicon. The deep offshore waters of the world have a fairly uniform salinity, at 34.7 parts per thousand. In other parts of the ocean, salinity varies. On the shallow flats of the Caribbean, for example, it reaches upward of 37 parts per thousand.

The biggest changes in salinity occur as you move closer to the coast, and especially into estuaries. Some species of saltwater game fish require full salinity in order to survive and thus are not found in these areas. Many other species of saltwater game fish can tolerate water where the salinity is only slightly diluted.

Striped bass are a wide-ranging anadromous fish.

As a rule, these predators will swim farther up inside the estuary on a flooding tide and stay farther downstream on the ebb. Bluefish do this in many coastal rivers, venturing upstream on a rising tide as far as salinity permits. Although most anglers are unaware of it, Atlantic bonito and little tunny do much the same in salt ponds and lagoons, riding into an inlet on the full salinity of a flooding current. At the top of the tide, they might be busting bait back in the pond along the edges of the channel. As soon as the current slows, however, they reverse their tracks and rapidly boogie back to the inlet and eventually open water.

Roughly 1 percent of the fish on our planet are capable of moving freely between fresh and salt water. These species are called diadromous. Of those fish, some, known as anadromous, migrate from salt water to fresh in order to reproduce. These fish can spend considerable time in fresh water, and some can even live totally landlocked. Furthermore, these species are incredibly hardy, fully able to travel hundreds and even thousands of miles upriver to spawn. Alewives, American and hickory shad, Atlantic and Pacific salmon, blueback herring, and steelhead are examples. Some of these precious migratory fish have become all too rare, so I urge you to let all wild anadromous fish go. Other species cross between fresh and salt water not to spawn but for food or shelter. These fish are called amphidromous. Tarpon, some silversides, sheepshead minnows, mummichogs, killifish, striped and white mullets, and white perch fall into this category. Amphidromous species typically spend little time in fresh water and rarely travel any major distance up a river.

WEATHER PATTERNS

Weather patterns have a profound impact on saltwater angling. Unstable weather, such as fronts and storms, produces unstable fishing. Either you're bailing fish one after the other or you can't buy a bite. Stable weather produces stable fishing. So if the fishing has been good, as long as the weather holds, the fishing is apt to remain that way. If, on the other hand, the fishing has been poor, you may need a change in the weather to get the action rolling. During the dog days of summer, fishing can be painfully slow, but the approach of a thunderstorm may suddenly make every fish in the neighborhood go on a feeding rampage, although you need to beware of lightning. Overall, optimal seasonal temperatures coupled with favorable winds and a steady barometer produce the most predictable and reliable fishing.

Rule Eleven: Fish in shallow water are very sensitive to changes in barometric pressure and the fronts associated with those changes. This seems especially true during times of year when water temperatures are marginal for the species you seek. So what can you expect? Cold fronts typically force fish to vacate shallow areas and move into deeper water. As a result, shore anglers groan and boat anglers grin. A warm front that arrives when water temperatures are just starting to climb into the fish's preferred range often accelerates the action. But a warm front that hits when water temperatures are at the high end of the fish's preferred range may shut down the

Changing weather produces changes in the fishing.

CAUTION

LIGHTNING STRIKE AREA

PLEASE SEEK COVER OFF THIS JETTY
PRIOR TO THE APPROACH OF STORMS.
INJURIES HAVE OCCURED ON THIS
STRUCTURE DUE TO LIGHTNING STRIKES.

Always take care to avoid lightning.

bite and force the fish to either go deep or feed at night.

Overcast skies and a light rain often hold very good fishing. But if the rain gets heavy and persists for more than a day, problems arise. Coastal rivers may discharge large volumes of discolored water. Turbidity in salt marshes will rise, and the salinity on large, shallow flats may be altered, driving game fish toward deeper water.

Perfectly calm days certainly make casting easy, and they also improve visibility for those involved in sight-fishing. But calm days also have their drawbacks. When the surface of the water is flat, fish are often less aggressive and very wary, quickly shying away from boat traffic noise and even wading anglers. So careful approaches are in order, and smaller flies seem to have the edge. Calm conditions either at night or in low light often bring fish to the surface, where they can be heard popping and swirling on bait. Not only does this make the fish easy to locate, but they are often very aggressive toward flies slowly dragged across the surface, such as sliders.

Foggy days are usually windless, and as on calm nights, fish commonly come to the surface. Granted, the fog makes it much harder to navigate a boat or even navigate on the beach, but if you can do it safely, it is well worth it. Look for swirls, wakes, fins slicing the surface, and busting fish. As with calm nights, try working flies right on top. They should be deadly. Oddly enough, foggy days can also hold opportunities for sight-fishing. Yes, fog reduces the light level considerably, but it also produces a very uniform, diffuse type of soft illumination, which results in little or no glare off the water. Coupled with the calm conditions, it may permit you to see cruising fish in shallow water.

A bit of wind—something on the order of 10 to 15 knots—generally makes the fish more aggressive and less wary, and thereby cranks up the fishing. A touch of disturbance on the surface can even enhance your sight-fishing by helping to hide your approach. As the wind gets stronger—15 to 20 knots—the fish become even more aggressive and harder to spook, although casting becomes an issue and sight-fishing goes out the window. If you can chuck a big fly in this kind of wind, by all means do it. Windy days attract big fish closer to shore, and these guys love to whack a big meal. Whenever there is a wind, the shorelines facing into it usually produce the most fish, since this is where plankton and forage fish concentrate.

BOAT TRAFFIC

Another factor that can have a noticeable effect on your fishing is powerboat traffic. Estuaries, particularly inlets and especially on weekends, are often loaded with these boats. One moment you see fish up on top happily munching bait; a powerboat roars by, and in a flash the fish are gone. Just as disconcerting, you might be paddling your kayak toward a bunch of busting fish, only to have a powerboat beat you there, leaving you rocking in its wake.

It makes excellent sense, therefore, to fish away from the main navigation channels and to plan your estuary fishing as much as possible during the off-peak hours. The low-light hours are an excellent choice in that regard. Not only will boat traffic be reduced, but this is the time when many predator fish are most active as well.

SAFETY

Rule Twelve: Be careful and use common sense. Because we are always near the water and are frequently in the open, anglers need to be careful about lightning. If the weather forecast calls for lightning, stay off the water. If you're fishing and see a lightning storm approaching, get off the water. And above all, don't stand in or near the water waving a graphite fly rod; you're just asking to be a target. For more information on lightning and how to avoid it, visit the National Lightning Safety Institute's website at www.lightningsafety.com.

Also take care to avoid duck hunters in season. Duck hunting is a popular sport in some coastal areas. Typically this is a late-fall activity and does not overlap with much of the fishing season. Nevertheless, duck hunters and anglers may find themselves on the same waters. Duck hunters usually operate from cleverly camouflaged sneak boats, plain tin boats, or shoreline blinds. Shoreline blinds are often semipermanent structures visible to the discerning eye. Note their position, and stay clear when duck season is open. Also avoid areas where decoys are set out.

CHAPTER TWO

Fly Rodding Salt Ponds and Lagoons

For the Atlantic saltwater fly rodder, salt ponds and lagoons are veritable gold mines. Not only are these locations sheltered from coastal wind and wave, but the water teems with marine life. Large schools of forage fish use these waters as nurseries and feeding grounds. And in response, large numbers of predator fish roam here as well. Sweetening the mix, salt ponds and lagoons are home to flats, and these frequently hold sight-fishing opportunities. Moreover, public access is generally good, and anglers find ample opportunities to fish from shore or a boat. Because of the sheltered nature of these waters, even a canoe, kayak, or rowboat can be employed.

A complete list of salt ponds and lagoons on the East Coast would quickly get unwieldy, but let me at least mention some of the best known. Lagoons with a reputation for excellent angling include Florida's Indian River Lagoon, which also contains the Banana River and Mosquito Lagoon; North Carolina's Pamlico Sound; New Jersey's Barnegat Bay; Great South Bay, Moriches Bay, and Shinnecock Bay, on the south shore of Long Island, New York; and Pleasant Bay, on Cape Cod, Massachusetts. Salt ponds deserving of mention are Winnapaug Pond, Quonochontaug Pond, Ninigret Pond, and Point Judith Pond, along the southwestern coast of Rhode Island; Great Salt Pond, on Block Island; Great Pond, Bournes Pond, Waquoit Bay, Popponesset Bay, and Cotuit Bay, on the south arm of Cape Cod; and Menemsha Pond, Lake Tashmoo, Lagoon Pond, and Sengekontacket Pond, on the north shore of Martha's Vineyard.

UNDERSTANDING SALT PONDS AND LAGOONS

Knowing the layout of any location helps you learn how to fish it. Salt ponds and lagoons are shallow estuarine embayments separated from the sea by a narrow strip of land called a barrier beach. The tide does not enter and exit these bodies of water freely but is instead forced to funnel through one or more restricted openings in the barrier beach. These openings are called inlets but may locally be known as breachways, cuts, or passes. Like all estuaries, these salt ponds and lagoons also have a source of fresh water. Typically the sweet water arrives via tidal creeks, which usually are located at the rear of the pond or lagoon, and often at the back end of a cove.

Salt ponds and lagoons differ only in shape and size. Lagoons tend to be long, narrow bodies of water running tight to, and parallel with, the mainland. Though they vary considerably in overall length, they are nevertheless large. The Indian River Lagoon is likely the longest on the Atlantic, snaking some 156 miles along the east coast of Florida. Pamlico Sound is nearly half that length, and Barnegat Bay is roughly a third of it, at about 45 miles in length, with an average width around 3 miles. Shinnecock Bay is much smaller, at close to 10 miles long and 3 miles at its widest point. Salt ponds are usually somewhat round in shape and are smaller bodies of water, better measured in acres than in miles. The ones

mentioned above on the Rhode Island shore range from roughly 50 to slightly over 1,700 acres. Menemsha Pond on Martha's Vineyard is 640 acres, Lagoon Pond is 538 acres, and Sengekontacket is 720 acres.

Regardless of the shape and size differences, salt ponds and lagoons are fished in much the same way, as both contain identical types of habitat. Certain portions of those habitats contain the most fish and the best fishing. These areas are the inlet and its adjacent waters, channels, islands, flats and bars, and shoreline structures such as points, coves, and tidal creek mouths. The inlet and its adjacent waters are the richest and most complex of these habitats, but fine opportunities also await the angler inland.

The lighthouse at the entrance to Barnegat Bay.

A South Carolina salt pond.

INLETS

Whether they're called inlets, breachways, passes, or cuts, these places supply some of the hottest fly rod action on the planet. Fact is, if I were forced to fish only one type of location along the entire coast, this would be it. Inlets typically are relatively deep, have swift-moving currents, and are home to huge schools of forage fish. Little wonder then that inlets produce predictable fishing. What's more, inlets are legendary for producing big fish, so if you're looking to bend the rod right into the corks, this place is for you. And to top it off, you have variety. Because the mouth is directly connected to the ocean, inlets hold more different species of fish than you'll find up inside a lagoon or salt pond.

Inlets come in two basic varieties: those held permanently open by man-made structures—typically stone jetties—and those that have been left in a natural state. Of the jetty type, Florida's Sebastian Inlet and New Jersey's Barnegat Inlet are well-known examples. This kind of inlet receives the most angling pressure, and there are several reasons for their enormous popularity. Generally they are close to population centers and therefore very convenient. They usually have a wide range of services nearby, including tackle shops, marinas, and public boat ramps. And perhaps above all, a good percentage of these inlets have excellent public access. In fact, you can drive right up to many of them.

Inlets without jetties are highly dynamic structures, ever vulnerable to the whims of wind, weather, and tide. Expect extensive shoaling, and expect these shoals to constantly grow, shrink, and relocate over time. Consequently, the fishing structure is subject to change, and anglers must relearn these places from time to time. Some of these inlets are navigable, and some are not. But even those that permit boat traffic are best left to experienced local captains, as these waters can be some of the trickiest on earth. New Jersey's Beach Haven Inlet and Chatham Inlet on Cape Cod fit the bill here.

In contrast to permanent inlets, these places are far less likely to be near any paved road, and many are remote by a mile or more. So fishing these spots frequently involves a long trek, the use of a four-wheel-drive vehicle, or travel by boat. Still, these inlets are a favorite of mine. These shorelines are far less crowded with anglers than those of permanent inlets, and they see only a fraction of the boat traffic. And along with the fine fishing, the surroundings are scenic and wild. All told, a wonderful combination.

A few of these inlets open and close with the turning of the calendar. To keep them distinct, I'll call them seasonal inlets. These inlets are typically very small and run only periodically. They may be, for instance, little more than a

Inlets without jetties are great places to fish, but they are often remote from any road. I used my kayak to reach this one.

stream of water gushing across a beach. In the spring after heavy rains, an inlet might be several feet wide and shin-deep, but in the heat of summer, it may be dry as a bone. Some seasonal inlets are opened once or twice a year by human endeavor. This is generally accomplished by a backhoe digging a trench through the dune in order to lower the water level in a brackish pond. In a few weeks to a month or so, the opening closes on its own. The opening of Edgartown Great Pond on Martha's Vineyard is an example. Of all inlets, seasonal ones get the least angling pressure. It's not because the fishing is poor; far from it. It's because they are few in number, open only periodically, and often located in difficult-to-reach places.

FISHING INLETS

Inlets are famous for powerful currents. And it should not be surprising that those currents control the fishing. So in order to fish an inlet, it is imperative that you're able to calculate when the current will run and when it will reverse. To do that, you must understand the difference between time of tide and time of current, as explained in the previous chapter. It's a key concept.

Game fish love to hang where fast currents come in contact with structure. In an inlet, structure often means holes and valleys in the bottom, but it also includes

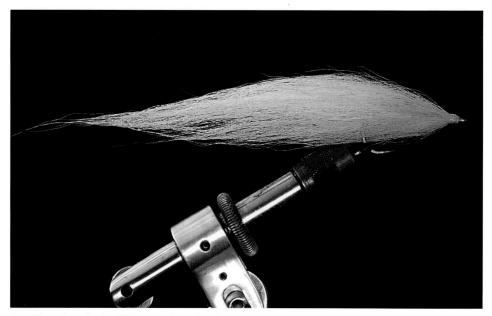

Big flies often fish well in an inlet. This fine pattern is Bob Popovics's Bucktail Deceiver.

drop-offs along a bar or the edges of the channel, the edges of a jetty wall, or any obstacle that breaks the current, such as a large rock or pier. Some of these structures may be too deep for you to see, but it is common for these deep structures to leave evidence of their existence on the surface of the water. Patches of turbulence, back eddies, and changes in the color of the water are the usual clues.

Another common surface clue is what anglers refer to as a seam. A seam is the intersection of slow- and fast-moving water. When the current is chugging through an inlet, you can expect it to create numerous seams, some of which may be 50 or more feet long. Seams usually are quite visible, and therefore easy to find, but here's one place to look: When the tide floods into an inlet, it usually forms a rip as it rounds the tip of the jetty wall. Typically this rip angles quickly away from the wall, leaving a band of slower water along the jetty. The interface where this band of slow water joins the rip is a seam.

In a deep inlet, these fish may be difficult to reach with a fly. And it's conceivable that in some cases, you simply won't be able to deliver a fly to the required depth, even at lower stages of the tide. Still, these deep haunts are where the biggest fish in the inlet are likely holding, so it's worth breaking out the sinking line and giving it a shot. Don't simply drop the fly on the structure and then retrieve it; instead, try the following things: Cast well upcurrent of the structure so your fly sinks and then swings over it. Also try casting across the current so the fly lands on the far side of the structure. Allow the fly to sink, and then retrieve so it passes in front of the structure. Repeat the cast, but this time get the fly to pass behind the structure.

Intermediate fly lines, or even floating lines, can be used successfully, but often it takes a sinking fly line to cover a seam well. Whichever line you opt for, try casting such that the fly lands in the faster water and then swings across the seam. If the seam runs a considerable distance—and many do—move along the shore or jetty, making additional casts so as to cover as much of the seam as possible. Next, see if you can position yourself so as to make a cast that permits the fly to be retrieved along the length of the seam. These are productive tactics.

One side of an inlet is likely to be far more productive than the other. The reason for this is that one side is apt to be closer to the better seams or closer to the better bottom structure. Since fly-casting range is limited, if you're fishing from shore this is an important factor. So one of your primary missions in learning how to fish any inlet is discovering which side of it to be on. Public access at times will limit your options, but if both sides of the inlet are accessible to you, you owe it to yourself to do the necessary research. Fish them both; figure out which one is best.

Inlet fishing has a very strong seasonal character. Water temperature and length of day trigger baitfish to migrate into and out of inlets at certain times of year. Not surprisingly, game fish migrations are closely tied to the same times of year. And it is during these migrations that the fishing is often at its red-hot best. In the Mid-Atlantic, when mullet move out of the inlets in the fall, they spark striped bass and bluefish into tremendous feeding frenzies. Bay anchovies and juvenile menhaden do the same farther north.

Now a few words on safety. Some places on the coast have well-deserved reputations for being home to wild water. Inlets are one of them. Some days they're a piece of cake, but don't let that fool you. In a matter of hours, a peaceful inlet can be transformed into maelstrom. Suddenly there are monstrous waves, pounding surf, and rips that pull with the strength of ten thousand locomotives. All it takes is a shift in the wind and tide. Never forget it.

With those fundamentals under your belt, you're ready to head to the water and start fishing. Inlets are complex, so to facilitate the discussion, they have been subdivided into three separate angling areas: the mouth of the inlet, where the waters of the salt pond or lagoon join the sea; the throat, the stretch of swift-

A school of juvenile sea herring migrating through an inlet.

moving water that connects the mouth to the pond or lagoon; and the inside corners, where the throat opens to greet the wider body of water.

Fishing the Mouth of an Inlet
Inlets with jetties
When fishing from a jetty, the basic procedure is to cast into the inlet, covering the current with a traditional down-and-across presentation. If you're lucky enough to encounter fish feeding on the surface, you'll know right where to begin. Ninety percent of the time, however, there are apt to be no visible signs. In such cases, target the two most likely holding areas: the deep water near structure and the seams.

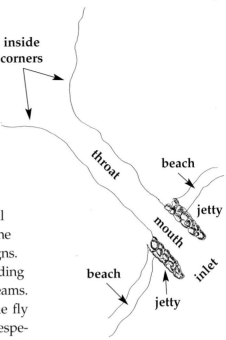

A strike is most likely to occur when the fly starts to swing back across the current, so be especially alert at that point in the retrieve. Similarly, when fishing a seam, be particularly on your toes as the fly begins to swing from fast- to slow-moving water. This is another moment when a strike may come. And don't drop your guard at the end

Inlets hold three main areas to fish: the mouth, the throat, and the inside corners.

of the retrieve. Game fish like to prowl near the edge of the wall, where the water drops away dark and deep. These fish have a habit of shooting up—seemingly out of nowhere—and grabbing the fly just as you're starting to pick it up for another cast. It frequently catches anglers by surprise.

Floating and intermediate fly lines can be effective, particularly in low light or any time the fish are feeding near the surface. Still, day in and day out, your bread-and-butter line in this location is a fast sinker. Game fish are frequently reluctant to swim up through heavy current to hit a fly. Therefore, it makes sense to deliver your offering to the fish's level. A 450-grain head on a 10-weight rod is a good choice, especially where large fish are expected. If fish greater than 10 pounds are unlikely in the area you're fishing, or if you simply need to use a lighter rod, try a 200-grain head on an 8-weight rod. It should do the trick. When using a fast-sinking line, avoid a long leader, since it allows the fly to ride upward in the water column. A short leader, in the 4- to 6-foot range, helps keep the fly downstairs, where the fish are.

Always give your sinking line ample time to descend before beginning the retrieve. To do that, a modification to the down-and-across presentation will work here, as well as in other places of swift water. Instead of casting directly across the current, angle your cast about 45 degrees upcurrent. Once the line lands on the water, hold the rod tip high, but do not retrieve. You can even throw some slack into the line at this point. The idea is to allow the line to freely sink as the current draws it back toward you. Once the line passes downcurrent of your position, lower the rod tip toward the water and quickly take up any slack. As soon as you're tight to the fly, begin the retrieve.

Throughout all of these tactics, there is one potential problem. When fishing down and across, many jetty anglers miss strikes. Here's why: Because you are standing above the water, it's easy to wind up with slack in the line between you and the fly. Be aware of this problem, and be ready to do something about it. The key thing is to keep the rod tip pointed down toward the water. To do otherwise pretty much guarantees missed strikes. Also realize that the higher above the water you stand, the more likely you are to have slack and the harder things become. So if you can safely climb down closer to the water and still have sufficient room for a backcast, do so.

Jetty walls offer a wide range of fish, including little tunny.

Here are two additional tactics that seem to produce when all else fails. The first involves retrieving a streamer along the jetty wall. Cast downcurrent so the fly lands about 15 feet or so out from the wall. Allow the fly a moment to settle, then retrieve it back along the rocks. After several casts, move ten steps along the jetty and cover new water. This presentation can be done with either a long or a short cast, and you can use either an intermediate or a sinking fly line. This same presentation can be applied in an upcurrent direction as well. Since the current is carrying the fly back toward you, however, you must strip line faster in order to stay tight to the fly.

The second tactic is a carryover from freshwater fly fishing. Using a strike indicator, try dead-drifting a fly along the wall or along a seam. This requires a floating fly line and a weighted fly such as a Clouser, Jiggy, or weighted shrimp pattern. The distance between the fly and the indicator is determined by the depth of the water. In general, you want to adjust it so the fly rides deep and almost out of view. Often that translates into 4 to 6 feet of separation.

Ideally, the fly should travel along the edge where the water drops off toward the channel. So cast upcurrent accordingly, and allow the fly to drift back toward you. You may have to mend the line and hold the rod high to get a natural drift. If you see a flash or the indicator goes under, set the hook. This is an interesting presentation that can be used not only in inlets, but pretty much anywhere you have current. (More details on this tactic can be found in chapter 4.)

All the tactics we have covered work on both the incoming and the outgoing current, although the outgoing typically produces the better bite. This is the stronger of the two currents and therefore more attractive to fish. Furthermore, on the outgoing current, schools of forage fish often set up shop right at the mouth of the inlet. Nevertheless, the incoming current can fish well and occasionally is the better bet. For instance, you may find that the fish are feeding well outside the mouth on the outgoing current, and unless you are in a boat, they might be beyond your casting range. On the incoming, those fish could come inside the mouth and be right at your feet. This is often the case with Atlantic bonito and little tunny.

Just as one side of an inlet often holds better fly rodding than the other, it is also common to find that some spots along a jetty wall consistently have hotter action than others. The reason is the same: They are closer to better structure and seams. To discover these spots, try various places on the jetty and make a mental note of which ones consistently produce. When you see other anglers hook up, note where they are standing. This is a time-consuming process, but it is absolutely the finest way to fully uncover a jetty's fishing potential. And once

Game fish often feed tight to a jetty wall.

you know the best fishing positions on a given jetty, you can gravitate immediately to them, skipping over the less productive areas and focusing your effort in places that count. Now your success rate will skyrocket.

The waters around the tip of the jetty are usually crawling with fish. Predators and prey tend to stack up in this vicinity, particularly on the ebb. Moreover, from the tip, you can cover a lot of water, casting in an arc of 270 degrees or more. Nice. Still, the tip of a jetty has its drawbacks. Out here, you're often eyeball to eyeball with other anglers. The seaward tip is nearly always home to the strongest wind and wave. And if the jetty is in disrepair, the tip may be difficult or even unsafe to reach. So take care.

The opposite end of the jetty, where it originates from the land , is another productive spot, often giving up the most fish on the incoming current. It is also far less crowded than the tip and is much easier to fish.

You can find additional hot spots by walking the wall and looking for schools of bait. Typically they will hold in particular areas where the current is to their liking. As you move along, eye the shape of the jetty. Some run straight as an arrow, but some have offsets and bends. Such features deflect the current, creating rip lines and back eddies, both of which usually host good fishing.

It's inevitable, especially after an hour or more of casting, that your backcast will occasionally drop down and touch the jetty wall. If you feel this happen, stop immediately and check two things. First, look to see if the point of the hook has been damaged. If so, sharpen the hook or change flies. Next, run your fingers along the leader, feeling for frayed spots. If you find them, repair the leader. Even if you don't feel your backcast touch, periodically stop and check things just to be sure.

The side of the jetty facing away from the inlet is worth covering, too. Currents are apt to be weak or nonexistent, but fish do feed here, especially when the wind is pushing against this side of the wall. The bowl formed where the jetty joins the beach is typically a collecting spot for many baitfish. Be sure to fish here; it is one of the best locations on this side of the wall. In addition, schools of bait regularly roam out of the inlet mouth and along the beach. As a result, the shoreline to either side of the mouth is home to some solid action. This is especially true in the fall as forage fish migrate out of ponds and lagoons for the winter.

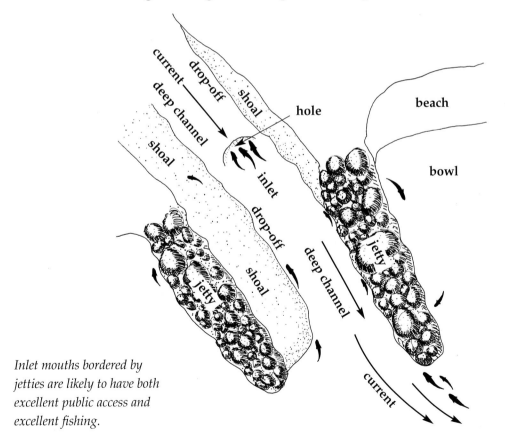

Inlet mouths bordered by jetties are likely to have both excellent public access and excellent fishing.

Jetty walls vary greatly in height, length, and condition. Consequently, the difficulty of fishing from a jetty wall varies greatly, and so do the risks. Make no mistake: It's entirely possible to fall down on a jetty or even fall in the water. And given the unforgiving materials that jetties are made out of, you might break a rod or even an arm.

How level the jetty is on top largely determines how hard it will be to navigate the wall. A few are nearly as flat and wide as a suburban sidewalk; most jetties, however, have a combination of easy and rough terrain. So move about slowly and with reasonable care. I strongly suggest purchasing a set of cleats. These are a wise investment for any jetty angler. Some jetties are little more than a pile of jagged boulders, capable of intimidating a goat. If you are going to take on these types of places, you need to be doubly careful. Here cleats are mandatory, and you should take a wading staff as well. This is a great aid in keeping your balance.

Wherever you take up station on a jetty, avoid standing on extremely uneven ground or on rocks that teeter under your weight. Both things are tiring and an invitation to a fall. Instead, pick the widest, flattest casting platforms you can find.

Expect the sides of a jetty to have slick rocks covered in seaweed and algae, especially down in the intertidal zone. And a low jetty, one that is largely submerged at high tide, may be slimy pretty much everywhere. This means that landing a fish from a jetty wall can be a real problem. Not only may the sides of the wall be steep and slick, but they may be awash in waves as well. Caution is the name of the game. Ideally, you could walk back to shore with a hooked fish in tow and then land it on the beach, but in reality, this is often not an option. Many jetties are quite long, and steering a fish to the beach could mean walking a hundred yards to a quarter mile over rough, uneven ground. Furthermore, your path may be blocked by other anglers, some of whom may also be fighting fish, or there may be a fleet of lobster buoys to maneuver around. Problems abound.

For these reasons, you or a friend may have to land the fish by climbing down the wall. Here are several ways to avoid injury. Wear the appropriate footwear, including cleats. Scout out the safest place to descend the wall before you begin casting. Take your time; no fish is worth risking a fall. If the wall is awash in waves, consider putting the rod down, grabbing the fly line, and hauling the fish up the rocks. Crude, yes, but if your tippet can take it, it's far safer. A long-handled landing net is extremely handy in these situations. With it, you will not have to descend the wall as far.

Occasionally your favorite jetty will have surf climbing the walls. Always size up the situation carefully before venturing out. If you elect to go out on the jetty anyway, go slowly and use extra caution. If you decide not to fish, make a mental note of the strength and direction of the wind. By doing so, you can predict these conditions in the future. For instance, a 25-knot southwest wind against the west wall at Point Judith is going to be trouble, but if you're fishing the north wall of Barnegat Inlet, it's the northeast wind that produces pounding surf.

Tide figures in, too. At higher stages of the tide, the surf may roar up the side of the jetty and then spray across the top in a mountain of white foam. Without foul-weather gear, you'll be soaked to the skin in seconds. The water may be flooding over the jetty as well. It's an exhilarating display of nature at work, but it can be very dangerous, even for highly experienced jetty anglers.

Inlets without jetties

Inlets without jetties present anglers with a slightly different set of challenges. First off, the lack of jetties means there is no permanent casting platform from which to cover the currents in the mouth. Now that may seem a serious downside, but the absence of jetties creates other opportunities. Because the inlet's currents are not contained between rock walls, they tend to be broken up into multiple rips and spread over a wider area. The currents are, in other words, more complex, and that complexity promotes the formation of complex bottom structure, such as sandbars and holes. Some of this structure may lie well out from shore and therefore be unreachable from shore. Commonly, however, much of it develops as a direct outgrowth of the shoreline itself and is relatively easy to cover either from the beach or by wading.

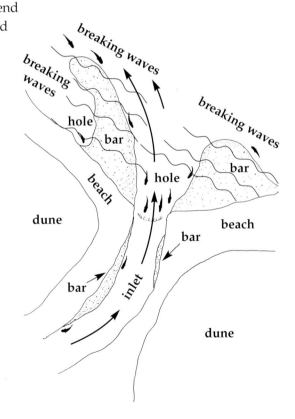

Finding this shoreline structure isn't hard, especially if you search around at the lowest stages of the

Without jetties, an inlet mouth is a dynamic place, ever subject to change. Still, the fishing is apt to be superb.

tide. Some bars are fully exposed at low water and are easy to locate and investigate. Yet even when submerged, bars can be spotted by the experienced eye. Where the water is clear, the changes in depth associated with a bar can be seen as changes in the color of the water. The shallow areas over a sandbar are lighter and tend to be yellow-green. The deeper water nearby is darker and bluer. If the water is turbid, look instead for breaking waves that indicate a shallow area or a bar. Rip lines, patches of turbulence, and seams are other good indicators of bottom structure.

After scouting out the major areas of bottom structure, explore them with a fly. Try them on both the incoming and outgoing currents; this will help you fully understand their fishing potential. While you're fishing these areas, look for patterns to emerge. As current speeds and water depths change from hour to hour, fish relocate, and thus areas of bottom structure tend to go hot and cold. Try to determine during what stages of the tide a given piece of structure fishes best and where the fish are likely to move next.

Pay special attention to places where the current crosses a steep slope in the bottom. Such spots are frequently found along the perimeter of a bar, where it drops away into a hole or depression in the bottom. Predator fish love to hang along this type of edge and in the rip lines that form here. Typically, the steeper the slope, the more productive this edge is apt to be, and the more likely large fish are to be found. The majority of the fish often sit along the drop-off where the rip first forms. Some of these fish may be quite deep, however, so a sinking line is in order. More than likely additional fish will be holding farther downcurrent. Look for them to be in areas of the rip that show the most turbulence on the surface.

Wading out on bars swept with current—particularly one bordered by deep holes—can be risky. The worst of these scenarios is found in inlets where the tidal range is 8 feet or greater, such as Chatham Inlet on Cape Cod. The currents in these inlets are enormously powerful, and making things even more dangerous, heavy surf may be crossing the bar as well. Use your common sense and the utmost discretion. If in doubt, back out.

As with jetties, schools of bait roam along the adjacent beaches. So if the bars and rips fail to give up any rewards, try hiking down the strand a bit. If you see no signs of feeding fish, immediately search for signs of bottom structure such as points and bowls, additional bars, and pockets of deep water. All of these may hold fish.

Seasonal inlets—especially those opening onto exposed ocean beaches—are home to plenty of bottom structure. Often right at the mouth is a hole, and don't let the small scale of these inlets fool you. This hole might be only 40 feet in diameter, yet it could well be over 20 feet deep. Down in the cellar of this inky blue water, there are apt to be some real tanks. And they might be there at any time of day, even high noon. Getting them to take a fly near the surface won't be easy, so your fast-sinking line should be employed. Because the currents here are not as swift as in a bigger inlet, delivering a fly deep is far less of a problem.

To the sides of such a hole, bars form extending out into the surf. If you watch the waves breaking as they come into shore, you'll get a good idea of the shape and size of these bars. Casting a fly out to them is effort well spent. Wading out onto these bars may be tempting, but it is a dangerous deed. In these situations, the waves may not only be large, but they may come at you from several different angles, and it is easy to get unexpectedly blindsided by a huge wave.

After covering the hole and the neighboring bars, work your way a short distance down the beach. Where the bars end to the right and left of the hole, they often slope away rapidly into deeper water. A good many fish may be sitting along those slopes. To find these fish, study the length of the breaking waves as they ride over the bars. You're looking for the end of the breaking wave where it tapers off into calmer water. Once you find it, cover this transition area well. A sinking line is certainly good, but a floating line and a popper or slider may be just as deadly.

Fishing the Throat of an Inlet

The mouth of an inlet offers superb fishing, no question. And for that reason, many fly rodders direct nearly all of their attention there. Don't be one of them. Right nearby is the throat of the inlet, with fine fishing potential and less crowded conditions. The throat is a confined stretch of water that connects the inlet's mouth to the pond or lagoon. It may be a quarter of a mile long, or it could be only 100 yards. Regardless, it is often filled with deep, fast-moving water and loads of bait, all of which means it's capable of holding plenty of game fish, and big ones at that. In fact, during the season, some big fish make these areas more or less their permanent residence.

The currents here may be even swifter than in the mouth of the inlet, and because of it, the fish are even more likely to stay glued to the bottom. That can be a real problem, for if the channel is more than 10 or 15 feet deep, even the fastest-sinking line may not be able to reach them. Consequently, the hours between the end of the outgoing current and the start of the incoming current are frequently a prime time to wet a line here. During this window, the current runs at its slowest pace, and the fish are free to rise off the bottom and feed near the surface, where they are easier to target with a fly. This includes even those monster-size fish that

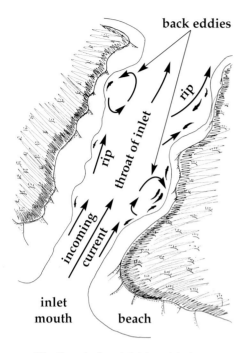

back eddies

rip

throat of inlet

rip

incoming current

inlet mouth

beach

The throat of an inlet is apt to have strong currents and deep water. Fast-sinking fly lines may be required.

seem to rarely ever chow topside. And as with so many angling opportunities, this one is at it finest when it occurs in periods of low light.

If Atlantic bonito or little tunny are your target, however, you'll do better on the incoming current. And in this part of the inlet, it's the last half of the incoming that seems to hold the most promise. The action often slows as the current wanes, but hold your ground. The fish that have gone farther up inside the inlet may well make a return trip by you shortly. Be patient.

These two fish are barn burners and can blow by you in the wink of an eye, so it is very important to stay focused and keep the fly wet. Many times the strike comes seconds before you actually see the fish arrive. Don't sit on the banks waiting for the fish to pop up; keep blind-

The throat of an inlet is productive and often less crowded. An angler prepares to release a little tunny.

The throat to Menemsha Pond on Martha's Vineyard.

casting. Pay attention to what is going on. Frequently these fish will attack selected areas of the inlet repeatedly. If you see that happening, position yourself within casting range.

Fishing for these two turbocharged guys may be different each day, so you have to adjust your tactics to fit. Some days the fish are blasting bait in the center of the inlet, and long casts are required to reach them. But on the incoming current, bands of bait often sit within 6 feet of the jetty wall or the banks of the inlet, and this is where all of the action takes place. When that seems the case, make only short casts that drop your fly in the middle of the bait. Keep doing it until the bonito and tunny roar by. On occasion you'll see the fish coming down the wall toward you, spraying bait. Holding your fire until the last moment and then slapping the fly down right in front of the fish as they appear can produce jolting strikes.

While you're fishing, keep an eye out for any indications of bottom structure. As in the inlet mouth, rip lines, seams, or patches of turbulence are always good clues, and all of them are common in this area. Also look for any irregular features in the shoreline. Where the shoreline meanders—either jutting outward or cupping inward—expect that there is bottom structure nearby worth investigating. If the inlet has a jetty, immediately inland of the jetty, where the rock and concrete end, you are apt to find an indentation in the shoreline. Typically this indentation adjoins a deep hole. It's a productive pocket, and one overlooked by many anglers. Fish feed here particularly during the incoming current.

Often the shoreline of the throat holds a series of indentations. Here you may find back eddies, places where the current circles on itself. As the current circles, it slows, permitting plankton to settle out. That attracts schools of baitfish to set up shop here. In response, game fish like to either periodically blast through these back eddies or lurk nearby in the shadows. Presenting a fly, however, is tricky. If your cast lays the line across currents going in opposite directions, the currents will quickly put slack in the line. When that happens, you lose control of the fly and will likely miss any strike. For that reason, I prefer to use short casts that target specific sections of the current. I also watch the path my fly takes, and if it is not the one I wanted, I change my position on the shore so the fly travels through the best-looking areas. Even with all this maneuvering, line control remains ever important; immediately try to remove any slack caused by the current.

Use extreme caution when fishing these areas. In the throats of these inlets, the shorelines can be exceedingly steep. In fact, it is possible at dead low tide to find yourself standing 10 feet above the water atop a 70-degree pitch. And at the base of that slide is a 25-foot-deep hole. At high tide, it may be possible to safely fish such a location, but at low water, stand well back or, better yet, pass it by.

The throat of a seasonal inlet may be little more than a stream of water cutting through the dunes. Even though it is a relatively small piece of water—perhaps only 15 feet across—the current here is still swift. As a result, the fish seek shelter from the force of the flow by hugging the bottom in the deeper sections. So concentrate on these deeper pockets, and the basic down-and-across presentation should work fine. As you move along, however, be aware that the banks are soft sand and undercut by the current. So it is very likely that they may collapse under your full weight. It is prudent, therefore, to stand back a bit, or be prepared to take a swim.

Fishing the Inside Corners of an Inlet

The final inlet opportunity occurs at the inside corners, where the throat joins the wider waters of the pond or lagoon. As in the mouth of an inlet without jetties, the currents here are complex, and as a result, bottom structure is created. In its simplest form, this may amount to shoals and bars on one or both sides of the main channel, but it could be quite a bit more elaborate. In larger salt ponds and lagoons, there might be two or more islands separated by winding channels. And these islands are apt to be surrounded by numerous bars, flats, holes, and submerged aquatic vegetation, such as eelgrass beds.

The inside corners are productive on both the incoming and outgoing currents, and they can hold some very big fish. As with all fishing locations, expect peaks and valleys in the action. During the last of the outgoing current, schools of game fish that have been feeding to the rear of the pond usually move back toward the inlet. As they do, they come through this area, giving you a chance to offer them a fly. The window of opportunity may be brief, however, as the fish can boogie by quickly on their way to the mouth of the inlet. In fact, you may get only thirty minutes of action.

For that reason, I prefer to fish these spots on incoming water. At that time, schools of baitfish stack up at the corners to feed on the food brought in by the tide. As they do, game fish are drawn here as well, and the action can be consistent over a longer period. During the first two hours of incoming current, the water level is still relatively low, and that offers several advantages. For one thing, you have more opportunities to wade. Also, the fish that set up on the corners early in the flood are often concentrated and very aggressive. Later,

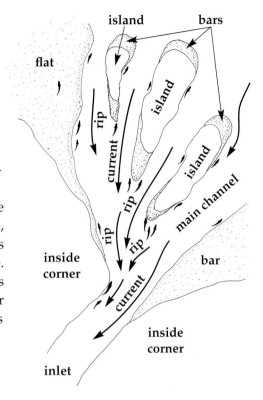

Compared to the mouth on an inlet, the inside corners see far less fishing pressure, yet there are plenty of fish here.

This bluefish is nearly 3 feet long and living proof that the inside corners of an inlet hold large fish.

An angler works the inside corners at twilight.

as the water level increases, the fish tend to disperse more and slowly head toward the rear of the pond. Another plus is the fact that during the hours of low water, powerboat traffic may be substantially lighter. This means feeding fish stay up longer and are less likely to spook.

As the water starts to rise, expect fish—such as striped bass and weakfish—to come up out of the channel and feed along its edge, eventually working their way out to the adjoining shallows and flats. It's possible that you'll be able to reach some of these "skinny" water areas by wading out from shore. If you do so, note that occasionally these shallows are separated from the shoreline by a trench of slightly deeper water. Take this added depth into account if the tide is incoming, or the return trip to shore may be wetter than you would like.

Game fish are creatures of habit. And that trait is reflected in the fact that when game fish move to or away from a feeding area, they like to travel the same route time and again. When fish come up onto a flat, that route is frequently a groove or trench in the bottom that connects the perimeter of the flat to deeper water. The fish may use this same travel lane to exit the flat on the ebb. As you might imagine, these travel lanes are excellent places for an angler to set up an ambush.

To find travel lanes, you need to be observant. A tour of the flat at low tide is apt to reveal likely locations, but better yet, stick around as the tide rises. Ideally, you'll see the fish actually arriving, but more likely what you'll see, at least initially, is how the tide progresses over the flat. That's a critical clue. Because travel lanes are depressions or grooves at the perimeter of a flat, these are the areas where the tide fills in first. In addition, these travel lanes frequently act as funnels, focusing streams of water up onto the flat. That makes them very easy to spot.

Unlike the flats farther back inside a salt pond or lagoon, these flats have fairly strong currents. So as the tide pushes up onto the flat, the travel lane may develop into a rip. This rip may run hard for only a short period of time, perhaps less than an hour. Still, rips are very attractive to schooling predators and prey, and these are no exception. In fact, a rip in this location may provide the hottest fishing the flat has to offer. So keep an eye out for them, and realize too that a rip may occur in these locations during the falling tide as water drains off the flat.

Additional rips may form as the tide rises higher on the flat. A common place to find one of these rips is where two flats of unequal height meet. The transition between them is usually a gradual incline, but I have seen flats meet

It often pays to work the edges of the channel, especially at lower stages of the tide and in the brightest part of the day.

The light-colored bottom in the foreground is about a foot higher than the rest of the flat. You can tell from the corrugated look of the bottom that a rip forms here on the incoming tide.

along a pretty sharp step in the bottom. Either way, the differential in heights causes tidal currents to pick up speed as they cross from one flat to the other. These rips may be quite broad, 50 feet or more, and therefore stick out like a sore thumb. Here again, a tour of the flat at low tide can be helpful in identifying likely places. Be especially suspicious of any area of a flat where the bottom has a corrugated appearance. These ripples, called swash marks, are evidence of swift current crossing over the bottom.

Move slowly as you wade across a flat; there may be fish close by and even some sight-fishing possibilities as well. If there do not seem to be any fish up on the flat, gradually work your way toward the channel's edge. Generally speaking, a floating or intermediate fly line is the right choice for flats work, but here at the channel's edge, a sinking line or at least a weighted fly will be very handy.

Stand near the drop-off, or if in a boat, anchor accordingly. Then try probing the edges of the channel. When on foot, take care, especially in estuaries where the water clarity isn't good. Navigation channels leading back into the salt pond or lagoon are commonly dredged to a minimum of 7 or 8 feet, so don't get so close to the drop-off that you could slip in. Fish holding in these channels are likely concentrated into small areas, which means that it pays to cast and move along the edge until you find them. It's worth the effort, as once you hook a fish, you may be able to hook several more in the same spot.

Where there are islands or flats separated from shore by deep water, a canoe, kayak, or rowboat is a real friend. You can fish from the boat, but I prefer to use it primarily for transportation. Although the use of a lightweight boat is risky in the mouth or throat of an inlet, which are often tricky waters with swift, occasionally rough currents and a lot of powerboat traffic, back in the inside corners, things are more protected, and such a boat can be used with care, especially during the hours when powerboat traffic is light. Pay attention, act prudently, and use common sense. Large motorized vessels passing through these areas can produce sets of waves that could conceivably capsize a canoe or kayak if hit broadside. Powerboats are often traveling fast and don't expect to encounter smaller, slower-moving boats in their path. This is similar to the situation bicyclists face when using a busy road; people driving cars are somehow blind to them. So it is imperative that you make your boat as visible as possible, and carry a horn to announce your presence to any vessel bearing down on you.

Once I reach a shallow area, I'll climb out and wade. That requires that you secure the boat so it doesn't drift off unexpectedly. To do that, you might pull

By positioning yourself near the channel's edges, you can often score. Here a fish is caught from my drift boat.

the boat up on dry ground or simply anchor it in shallow water. In either case, figure out what the tide is doing. If you pull the boat up only a short way and don't bother to use an anchor, a rising tide could set the boat afloat without warning. If you anchor it on a short rope, a rising tide could cause the boat to pull the anchor free. If you wander off a long way during a rapidly falling tide, you may turn to see your boat higher and drier than you wanted, leaving you with the unpleasant task of dragging it to the water's edge.

Here's another idea, one I use from time to time. Carry a long rope on board. After exiting the craft, tie one end around your waist and the other end to the bow. Now you can wade along, towing the boat behind you. This may sound awkward, yet it often works well, particularly with a lightweight, shallow-draft boat. Moreover, it can be very convenient. If you suddenly discover that you need something stored onboard, such as additional flies, food, or water, you just haul the boat to you.

FISHING A SALT POND OR LAGOON

As you move farther back into the pond or lagoon, the waters widen and take on the look of a lake. Channels, flats, and islands exist here too, but the currents are much slower and the fish are more spread out, so you can't expect the kind of concentrated and consistent action found at the inlet. Still, fine fishing opportunities exist, and there are a few bonuses thrown in as well. Back here the opportunities to wade greatly increase, and along with them, opportunities for sight-fishing. And because there is less current and boat traffic to contend with, a canoe, kayak, or rowboat can really come into its own. But best of all, it's a whole lot easier to find quiet, undisturbed water where you can wet a line in peace. I like that.

Navigational charts quickly reveal that salt ponds and lagoons are predominantly shallow. In fact, it is common for a large percentage of their total area to have a mean low water depth of 4 feet or less. And in some cases, healthy-size chunks of the bottom are fully exposed at dead low tide. These flats are far bigger than the ones you find at the inside corners. One thing remains the same, however: Travel lanes are still a key part of the game.

When fish enter and exit the extensive flats inside a salt pond or lagoon, they are apt to do so using established travel lanes. No surprise there. Given the size of these flats, however, there may be more than one entrance and exit. And there are probably additional travel lanes up on the flat itself. Why? A school of feeding fish must comb these extensive shallows in search of food. But it's

A small salt pond is an intimate piece of water.

unlikely they will do it haphazardly. Rather, schools of fish cruising a flat tend to do it by following changes in bottom contour; in short, they have preferred routes. None of this is to say that feeding fish only or always use those routes, but because they are creatures of habit, they do so with enough regularity that anglers can take advantage of it.

Where there are numerous adjacent flats, schools of game fish may feed on them sequentially during a single tide. They cruise one flat, grab what food is available, and then head to the next. Here again, these fish are likely to develop travel lanes by which they move from one flat to another, and these routes are likely to follow changes in bottom contour. In addition, the fish may visit the various flats in a particular order. For example, in these situations, it is common for them to go from a deeper flat to a shallower one as the tide level rises, and then reverse that direction as the tide ebbs.

It boils down to this: The bigger the flat, the more there is to know about how fish move on it. It also means that observant anglers, those willing and able to unlock those patterns, are going to be far more successful. Watching fish first-hand always provides the finest information. So when you see a school of fish cruise on or off or over a flat, note the location and the stage of the tide. Carry a notepad and pencil if it makes life easier. Revisit the flat at another time and see

Where several flats adjoin, fish tend to move from one to the next following the progress of the tide.

if that pattern of movement repeats itself. In a few weeks' time, you'll be surprised by what you have learned.

Beyond watching how fish behave on a flat, you should be familiarizing yourself with two additional things: the bait and bottom structure. Learning what types of bait are present will greatly assist you in selecting the right flies. Many of the lagoon flats of the Northeast are dominated in June by two types of baitfish: juvenile sand eels and juvenile sea herring. Both form large schools, often appearing as dark clouds moving across the bottom. The individual sand eels are tiny and require a small, thin fly to properly match. The juvenile sea herring are considerably bigger and wider, however, and a small, skinny fly is the wrong ticket. Knowing that kind of thing puts you ahead of the game.

Although the word *flat* implies that the bottom is perfectly uniform, in reality the bottom of a flat never is. All of them contain some unevenness. Granted, these variations in the bottom are relatively subtle; they may be minor depressions, trenches, and valleys. Yet fish do relate to them. While you're investigating the flat, take note also of dark patches of submerged vegetation such as eelgrass. Eelgrass beds are frequently found inside salt ponds where wave and current levels are reduced. This vegetation creates a hiding and feeding area for many forage items, from small baitfish and shrimp to immature squid. Naturally, this makes vegetation beds magnets for predators as well. Striped bass and weakfish, for example, are notorious for haunting eelgrass beds.

Besides holding food, these patches of vegetation offer game fish something else—camouflage. In fact, game fish gravitate to darker sections of the bottom in an effort to conceal themselves. And it doesn't have to be vegetation; a pile of rocks on an otherwise open sand bottom does the trick. From these hideaways, game fish watch the adjacent lighter bottom for schools of bait to swim by. For that reason, if you're wading or drifting over a light-colored flat and see a dark patch of bottom ahead, try throwing the fly there. And if the dark area is fairly large, try retrieving your fly along the edge where the light and dark areas meet.

Many flats have holes associated with them, and game fish love to sit inside them. Typically these holes take one of two forms. The first type is a shallow basin located on the flat itself. It may be no more than a couple of feet deeper than the surrounding flat and only 6 feet or less in diameter. Even when water clarity is high, these basins can be hard to see on an all-sand bottom. On flats

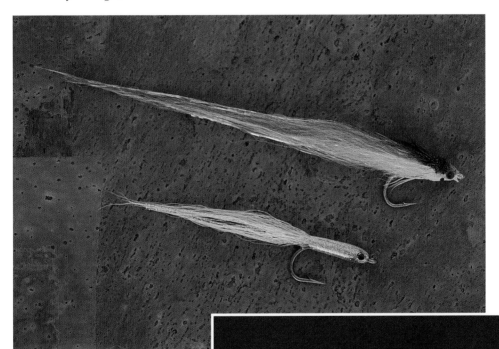

Above: *There are plenty of patterns to mimic sand eels. Here are two of them. On top is Bob Lindquist's Sand Eel Muddler, and on the bottom is Chris Windram's Epoxy Minnow.* Right: *In the spring, juvenile sand eels are a plentiful bait of northeastern ponds and lagoons, and you should have flies to match them.*

Flats are never perfectly flat. As this picture shows, the bottom has subtle shapes, valleys and ridges that fish relate to.

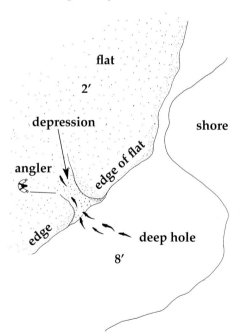

At dead low tide, fish tend to exit flats and then congregate in the nearest deep hole. As the tide starts to rise, expect these fish to return to the shallows.

covered with dark aquatic vegetation, such as eelgrass or turtle grass, the hole is usually barren of growth and stands out visually as a light-colored area on the bottom. Fish may be sitting either in the basin or just off its edge, especially if the basin is rimmed by darker-colored bottom vegetation. A cast to the perimeter of the hole is your initial step, and if that doesn't bring a strike, try casting so the fly travels right through the basin itself.

The other type of hole to look out for is a large one joining the perimeter of a flat. These holes can be significantly deeper than the neighboring shallows, at 6 feet deep or more, and they may be 30 feet or more in diameter. They provide a convenient resting place for game fish exiting the flat during the lowest stages of the tide, as well as a place for schools of fish to hide when spooked off the flat by recreational boat traffic. And last but hardly least, the biggest fish in the area will use these dark depths as a sanctuary.

At dead low, probe these deep holes with a sinking fly line. It can be plenty productive. While doing it, be on the lookout for packs of fish cruising the edges of the hole. Game fish often do this—sometimes circling the hole repeatedly—in preparation for moving back up on the flat. If you see such behavior, deliver your fly just ahead of the fish. As the tide starts to rise, these fish are likely to ride out of the hole and up onto the adjacent shallows. Expect them to leave in a line and disappear quickly, however. Prepare for this by switching to a floating or intermediate line and scanning the perimeter of the hole for a likely travel lane.

SIGHT-FISHING TACTICS

With shallow, clear water and sandy bottoms, salt ponds and lagoons are ideal sight-fishing destinations. You need the right weather conditions, however, to make sight-fishing possible. Sunny, bright skies are a major plus, providing the light you need to see. It's a real help if the sky is fairly free of clouds, since they are reflected in the water surface as glare. The best days are also fairly calm, since wind will disturb the surface and reduce visibility. Totally calm conditions may, however, work a bit against you. When the water is dead flat, the

Sight-fishing can be done from the bank.

As fish feed on a flat, you may see fins, tails, or flashes of silver. In the upper left third of the picture, a striper flashes as it feeds on sand eels.

fish tend to be spookier. Therefore, a tiny touch of breeze can help you hook up. Odd how that works.

You can sight-fish in one of three ways: from shoreline, by wading, or from the deck of a boat. The boat method is the easiest for many reasons. You're more mobile and therefore can quickly search several flats for the best bite. You can cover flats inaccessible on foot or too deep to be easily waded. And to top it off, when standing on the deck of the boat, you're much higher above the water and thus can see fish from a much greater distance. It makes all the difference in the world, and for this reason, some wading anglers carry a small stepladder or a plastic milk crate out onto the flats. These things boost your height and boost your hookups, although you need a fairly firm sand bottom to use them safely.

Sight fishing has its own blend of required skills. First and foremost, you need to be able to spot fish. Occasionally it's a piece of cake. In very shallow water, tails and fins sticking through the surface are fairly easy to spot, particularly in the right light. And a wake moving across the flats can be seen at a great distance. Fish actively feeding are not very discreet either. Swirls are an obvious clue, but you may also see a flash of silver as a fish turns on its side to grab prey. It's the same thing a freshwater angler sees when a trout rolls to take a nymph.

The real trick is the ability to see fish before they see you. Even in gin-clear water, at first that can be difficult. Don't expect to actually see the fish well. It can happen, but not as much as anglers would like. What you typically see amounts to little more than a narrow shadow moving across the bottom. Certainly, having the right light is a big help, but there are several other factors. Water clarity and depth play roles as well. The shallower the flat and the more transparent the water, the easier those fleeting shadows are to see. A light-colored bottom—which fortunately most flats have—is another huge plus. Polarized sunglasses and a long-brim hat are significant aids; in fact, they're really a necessity. And it helps greatly to have the sun at your back. Still, there is one

Above: *Unless conditions are perfect, it can be hard to see fish even in shallow, clear water. Here twenty or so striped bass fan out to feed on a flat.* Right: *Sometimes you don't see the fish until they are very close. These large stripers are only several feet away.*

more thing: You must learn not to watch the surface of the water, but to look for movement on the bottom. Train your eyes deep, right on the sand.

Once you have spotted fish, you must be able to cast quickly and accurately. Accuracy requires practice, practice, and more practice. Speed can also be improved by practice, but it is a factor of preparation as well. It is imperative that when the fish pull into view, you have enough line off the reel to reach them. How do you know how much is enough? You can only cast to fish within the range of your sight. And that range depends on the present conditions. So pick a target at the extent of your vision and cast to it. That is likely the maximum amount of line you'll need that day.

Next, organize that amount of fly line. To fire off a quick cast, you need to have some fly line already outside the rod tip. That translates into roughly 15 feet of line plus the leader. The exact amount is determined by your casting ability, the length of your leader, and the type of fly line you're using. For instance, short bellied fly lines and short leaders may require less. Practice on the water and you'll find out. If you're wading, you can simply drag this line along behind you; hold the rod tip up so the fly doesn't snag on the bottom. On shore or on a boat, holding the rod tip up is a good idea too, but also hold the fly in your hand. This is done by grasping the bend of the hook between the thumb and first finger, while allowing the point of the hook to be free and pointing away from you.

What about the remaining fly line? On a boat, you can simply lay it on the deck. If you're standing on shore, you can hold it in loops or lay it on the ground. If you're wading, you can hold the line in loops or drop a floating line to the water. Yet in all three situations, the safest and most effective method is to use a stripping basket. A fly line lying on the deck has a nasty habit of getting caught underfoot, and a line lying on shore snags all kinds of things. Loops work to some degree, but they can tangle big time. Hence, a stripping basket is the least of all evils.

Wading anglers are usually at the mercy of the tide. In many instances, they find themselves restricted to fishing a flat during the hours of lowest water, which in turn correspond to the first half of the flood and the final hours of the ebb. Without a doubt, both of these periods are often productive. Still, in my experience, the fish on a flat are most aggressive to the fly during the early hours of rising water. Not only are they hungry and eager to find food, but they are coming toward you and make it easy to present the fly. By the time the ebb rolls around, these fish have fed for several hours and are getting ready to leave for deeper water. In addition, they are more apt to be moving away from you, making it harder to present the fly.

The Right Presentation for Sight-Fishing

Even locally proven fly patterns may get repeated refusals. The issue is this: When sight-fishing, how you present a fly is at least as important as what fly you present. In fact, I would go so far as to say that presentation is the more important of the two. Regardless of what fly you pick, it must be shown to the fish in a way that provokes a strike. There is no way around it. And the presentation that works one day may fail the next, so you may have to do some daily experimenting to find what the fish respond best to. Nevertheless, there are some basic tactics you need to be aware of.

Presentation has two key aspects: placement and retrieve. Flats anglers typically deliver a fly in several ways. The classic sight-fishing method is to place the fly several feet ahead of the fish, and then allow it to sink to the fish's level or below

Above: *A Half & Half is a cross between a Clouser and a Deceiver. Tied sparsely, it is an excellent flats fly. This one is 3.5 inches long on a size 1 hook and can be easily cast on a 7-weight rod.* Right: *Crab flies are fish getters. These two Green Diablo crabs were tied by Alan Calo. They sport dumbbell eyes and ride hook-up.*

Sight fishing is a challenge, but when you do everything right, rewards—like this striped bass—come your way.

before starting the retrieve. Why? Even though the water is shallow, the depth at which the fly runs is usually critical to your success. Fish on a flat at times do take a fly moving overhead. Still, often these species are actively searching for forage either at their own depth or on the bottom. Consequently, their attention is often focused forward and downward, and any fly not in that zone may be ignored.

The exact distance to lead the fish is a factor of how fast the fish is moving toward you. The faster the fish, the farther ahead of it the fly must land. The type of fly line you are using and the weight of the fly are factors too. If the flat has a strong current running over it, that is a consideration as well. It may also mean you need a heavier fly, one that sinks quicker.

You can also try dropping the fly practically on the fish's nose. As soon as it lands, immediately start retrieving. Often this triggers an instinctive strike. Try this method when you see

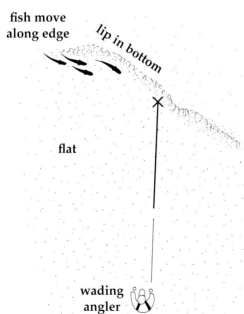

fish move along edge

lip in bottom

flat

wading angler

Flats are never totally flat. Instead, expect the bottom to have subtle ridges and depressions along which fish frequently travel. If you can position yourself near one of these lanes, you'll likely score.

a school of traveling fish. Quickly pick up the line and fire the fly right in front of the lead fish. Two or more fish may charge the fly. When fish are in a wary mood, however, this presentation can easily spook them.

The last method is to cast out into an area where you feel fish are likely to appear. Perhaps you know the area well, or you may simply see fish approaching off in the distance and have an idea of the route they will take. Either way, you cast out and allow the fly to sink to the bottom, and then wait for the fish to arrive. When they get within range, you start your retrieve. This presentation can be very deadly and often fools even the wariest fish.

Sight-Fishing Retrieves
A few types of prey, such as shrimp and amphipods, swim so poorly that a dead-drift presentation is best. Still, the majority of things that game fish eat are highly mobile, and as a result, predators expect their food to react in one of two ways: Either it flees for the next county, or it runs a short distance and then dives to the bottom in an attempt to hide. In order to make your fly look alive, you need to mimic these behaviors. Striped bass, for instance, follow a slow retrieve out of curiosity, sometimes coming practically to your rod tip, but they are rarely inclined to strike. It just doesn't look like natural behavior to them.

A moderate to fast retrieve matches the flight behavior of prey nicely and can easily be accomplished either with a one-handed strip or by placing the rod under your arm and using a two-handed strip (both of these retrieve styles are described in chapter 5). When all goes well, the fish charges the fly and strikes hard. I suggest starting the day with a moderate-speed retrieve, and if the fish follow but refuse it, gradually increase the speed on subsequent casts until you get a fish to strike. Weighted or unweighted patterns may be used, with a typical fly being a Clouser Minnow or a Lefty's Deceiver 2 to 4 inches in length. On occasion, a big fly of 6 inches or more cranked at breakneck speed works like magic. This tactic can save the day, and it is very effective on the larger fish on the flats.

To simulate the "run and hide" behavior, you'll want a weighted fly. I suggest crab and sand eel patterns, since both of these prey species exhibit this type of response to predators. Of the two, I use the sand eels more often. More specifically, I often rely on a sparsely tied half-and-half. If you're unfamiliar with this fly, it's simply a Deceiver tied with a Clouser-like lead eye at the head. So it's half Deceiver and half Clouser, hence the name. I like long, thin hackles; I find that this gives the fly more action and thereby triggers more strikes. Tied on a size 2 hook, this fly can be upward of 4 inches overall and still be light enough to deliver on a 6-weight fly rod.

As you wade a flat, you stir up the bottom, creating what is called a "mud." This "mud" attracts fish, so occasionally turn and fire a cast into it.

Retrieve the fly a short distance—3 to 5 feet—and then stop, permitting the fly to settle to the bottom. If the fish does not follow, repeat the motion in an attempt to attract the fish's attention. Fish that do follow may strike while the fly is moving or suck it in while it rests on the bottom. The first kind of take is easy to feel, the second type more subtle. If the fish tips head-down over the fly as it sits motionless, get ready. If the line draws tight, strike. If you even suspect the fish may have it but you are not sure, slowly slip-strike with the line. If you feel the fish's weight, strike hard. If there is no resistance, let the fly settle again.

ISLANDS

Up inside a salt pond or lagoon, you'll occasionally find one or more islands. And in some cases, there are enough islands to form a maze. Wherever these islands exist, the surrounding waters are commonly home to significant amounts of bottom structure, including flats, bars, holes, and weed beds. And even though the tidal currents are not as strong here as they are down near the inlet, bands of moving water and rip lines do exist. Little wonder then that these islands are frequently very fishy places.

Let's look at a classic example. One of the most productive islands to fish is one located just inside a barrier beach. Typically, this how they are set up: The island is longer than it is wide, with its long axis parallel to the barrier beach. Separating the island and the barrier beach is a passage of relatively swift current. There is also apt to be considerable depth here and possibly a navigation channel as well. The opposite side of the island has some small rips but in general has slower currents and broad shallows. The end of the island farthest from the inlet is somewhat blunt and featureless. The end closest to the inlet tapers to a point, and from this point runs a bar with rip lines and deep holes.

If you're lucky, the island is connected via a bridge to the mainland or to the barrier beach. Where that is the case, you can access the fishing by car or on foot. More often, however, this fishing requires a boat. So here again a canoe, kayak, or rowboat is a valuable tool. Don't attempt to cross navigation channels during busy times or during rough conditions, and always wear a life jacket.

Islands are often surrounded by complex bottom structure and currents.

The side of the island facing the barrier beach is likely to host bigger fish and the most fish as well. Floating and intermediate fly lines work well here at times, but the swifter currents and greater depth mean that fast-sinking fly lines are best in the long run. Even though you see broad areas of current, don't expect the fish to be equally spread out. As always, fish in a current tend to associate with areas of strong bottom structure. So you must study the surface for rip lines and areas of turbulence that indicate the existence of structure. This definitely will pay off. Do your job and you can catch five or more fish from one spot.

The far side of the island—the one holding slower water—has few fish but has its own special character. For one thing, this side may have far less boat traf-

Islands typically develop bars with steep drop-offs. These are excellent places to fish. This one is in Florida's Mosquito Lagoon.

fic, so it's quieter and more peaceful. You're less likely to need a sinking line, and there may be some sight-fishing opportunities as well. As you fish, expect that no one spot will hold a great many fish. Rather, you're likely to catch a fish here and a fish there. So plan on casting and moving. Focus on available structure, such as flats, drop-offs, holes, eelgrass beds, or oyster or mussel bars.

FISHING SHORELINES

Predator fish relate to structure, and the single longest continuous piece of structure is the shoreline itself. That's right, shorelines hold plenty of fish—it's something that shore anglers can attest to. Back up inside a pond or lagoon, most of this shore fishing centers around coves and tidal creek mouths. These two types of structure are covered in later chapters, but a few thoughts about these shorelines are appropriate here.

Public access to shorelines around the inside of a pond or lagoon is usually somewhat limited due to private development. There are areas inside these bodies of water, however, where it is difficult to build, and these locations provide anglers with opportunities to fish. These areas typically include the backside of the barrier beach, areas adjacent to the inlet, and wetlands to the rear of the pond. Parks and public boat ramps provide additional room too. If you have a boat, you can reach shorelines inaccessible to the angler on foot. Always respect public property.

Shoreline fishing can be good during the day, and some sight-fishing potential exists. Still, the best shore bite often occurs in low light. In darkness, many fish feed at or near the surface. This is particularly true of striped bass and weakfish, and on a calm night, it is common to hear them making popping sounds as they suck in bait. Any area of the pond illuminated by artificial light is apt to be especially productive, since the light attracts plankton and baitfish to the top, which in turn attracts game fish. Aided by the light, you are apt to see swirls as well, further helping you establish the position of the fish.

Shorelines brushed by current produce best. If you see or hear fish feeding, position yourself upcurrent of the activity, and make a cast across the flow such that the fly swings into the location where fish are active. During the swing, you may want to retrieve line slowly. This removes some of the slack from the line and permits a more positive hook set. Always hold the rod tip low to the water. This reduces slack too. And finally, strike with the line, not the rod tip.

When fishing the back shoreline of a salt pond or lagoon, try to find one or more tidal creek mouths. Though some may be found in a straight section of shoreline, they are far more likely to emerge at the rear end of a cove. Wherever you find them, tidal creek mouths have plenty of current and are loaded with plankton and baitfish, so the fishing here is usually excellent.

CHAPTER THREE

Fly Rodding Bays and Coves

Bays and coves are a near universal feature of the coast and are especially prevalent in New England. In geological terms, many of these are ancient river mouths that were submerged eons ago by a rising sea. And for that reason, you typically find one or more rivers entering at the head of a bay. Besides those found facing open water, bays and coves are also numerous in salt ponds and lagoons. Generally these are smaller, shallower structures, but like their larger coastal cousins, they are frequently connected to a source of fresh water, in this case, a tidal creek or stream.

For our purposes, we'll define a bay or cove as a notable indentation in the shoreline. In terms of size, they cover quite a range. A cove might be a U-shaped section of shoreline in the rear of a salt pond, barely 200 feet across. An angler could quickly cover such a place in less than an hour's time. Bays and coves on the open coast, framed by rocky headlands, are considerably larger, their lengths and widths often measured in miles. At the extreme far end of that spectrum are places such as Chesapeake Bay and Narragansett Bay, enormous bodies of water filled with numerous coves, river mouths, islands, and uncountable fish haunts. An angler couldn't hope to fully learn either one in a lifetime.

UNDERSTANDING BAYS AND COVES

Bays and coves, unlike salt ponds and lagoons, have wide mouths connecting them to open water. No narrow inlets here. That means the current patterns in bays and coves are neither as localized nor as swift. Rather, the tide enters and exits these bodies of water in a more generalized fashion. Consequently, bay

A bay on Cape Cod, Massachusetts.

fishing can be spread out. Some days the fish roam all over the place, seemingly without rhyme or reason. And when that happens, it's hard to get a fly in front of them. Nevertheless, those areas in the bay that do hold current—regardless of how weak—are the keys to consistent success. Here prey and predators are far more likely to hold, and your odds of a hookup increase accordingly. So the time and effort you put into understanding how the water moves through a bay are well spent.

Another thing that distinguishes coastal bays and coves from salt ponds and lagoons is water depth. Ponds and lagoons are overwhelmingly shallow structures loaded with flats. Although many bays and coves contain flats, they may account for only a small percentage of the total area. Instead, bays and coves, particularly those in the Northeast, often have fairly deep water and therefore do not warm as quickly or cool as rapidly as salt ponds and lagoons. So the fishing season is apt to start later in the spring and last longer into the fall. And where bays have great depth, they may even contain fish that winter over.

There are, however, some very shallow coves, especially inside salt ponds and lagoons. Here the water depth may average less than 5 feet at high tide and under a foot at low. Because of the limited depth, the fishing here is often confined to higher stages of the tide. These shallow coves undergo relatively wide swings in water temperature. On a hot summer day, the water temperature may soar, causing game fish like weakfish or striped bass to remain outside the mouth much of the day, entering the cove only during the cool hours around midnight. In late fall and early spring, these shallow coves cool down on clear, cold nights, and the fishing may be restricted to the warmest part of the day.

Because bays have open mouths, wind can be a major influence in pushing and concentrating plankton. As a result, the shoreline that faces into the wind is where the plankton and baitfish often stack up. So don't be surprised if the hottest action a bay has to offer takes place where the wind drives directly onshore. It happens a lot, particularly in the spring and fall, when the wind is at its strongest of the year. The open mouth of a bay also means that salinity typically remains fairly high, permitting species like Atlantic bonito and little tunny to feed here at all stages of the tide.

FISHING IN COASTAL BAYS AND COVES

Fish feeding in bays and coves are occasionally in plain view. Given that fact, it's critical, as it is when fishing in ponds and lagoons, that you systematically scan the surface for signs of active fish. Swirls, slicks, spraying bait, diving birds, fins and tails, or patches of nervous water are the common clues. You'll find these signs of fish on top all too rarely, however; more often than not, the fish will be deep and hidden from view. To be regularly successful in bays and coves, you must know how to hunt down your quarry. Zeroing in on the fish is the single most important skill a saltwater fly rodder can learn.

When hunting a shoreline, there is one cardinal rule to apply, no matter where you go: Locate the prime real estate—those areas with bottom structure and current. This is the habitat that holds predators and prey. If you're wading, especially in clear water, you'll feel the current around your legs, and bottom structure such as holes, drop-offs, and bars will be plainly visible. Where the water is too deep to wade, however, you're forced to investigate matters from a distance. That requires a higher level of skill, although that level is not difficult to attain.

To find structure and current from a distance, focus your attention on two things: the surface of the water and the shape of the shoreline. Where there is current or structure, the surface of the water often records that fact. Scan the surface for anything that appears out of the ordinary. Fast-moving water usually appears much darker than the surrounding area and kind of lumpy, and because of it, a rip stands out quite a ways. Where a strong current goes around a stationary object, such as a boulder, you'll see patches of turbulence and back eddies. Slow-moving current is subtle and harder to see. Try to determine the direction in which floating objects drift or the way lobster pots or buoys lean.

Current and bottom structure nearly always go hand in hand. So once you find one, start looking for the other. Current is easy to see and can be felt along your legs or observed in the swing of your fly line. Bottom structure can be harder to detect. Most structure involves a change in water depth, and a change in depth is often made visible by changes in either the color of the water or how waves behave. Deep areas look darker than shallow areas. Over a light sand bottom, the effect is most pronounced. Blue areas are the deepest, green areas

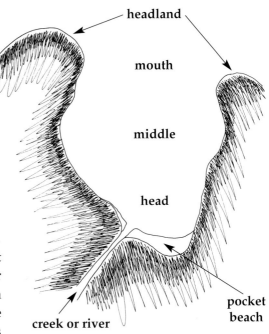

Think of a bay as made of three pieces: the mouth, the middle, and the head. All of them hold promise.

are less deep, and yellow areas are shallow. As waves move from deep to shallow, they tend to heighten. If the bottom is very shallow, the waves will then break. This is a common clue to the presence of a bar.

The shape of the shoreline is a very valuable clue in your hunt for fish, as it is an indication of the shape of the adjoining bottom. Sections of shore that run in a straight line typically have uniform bottoms and lack much structure or current. As soon as the beach twists or turns, or bulges in or out even slightly, the picture instantly changes. The more irregular the shape of the beach, the more irregular the adjoining bottom. This is where you'll find structure and current, and it's where the fishing is likely best.

This relationship between the shape of the shoreline and the presence of bottom structure makes it much easier to detect submerged structure, which can be difficult to see, while the shape of the shoreline is in plain view. It's merely a matter of taking the time to do it. Furthermore, you can use this method on a small or large scale. The more irregular the shape of an entire bay or cove, the more bottom structure it contains and the more places there are for fish to feed.

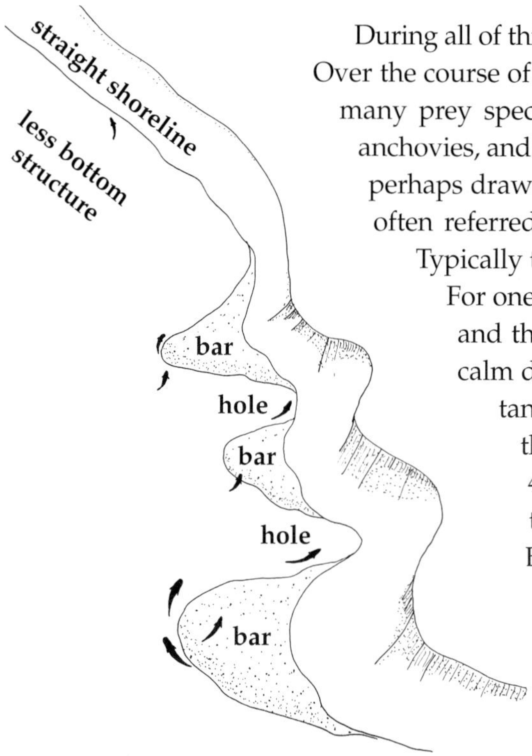

straight shoreline

less bottom structure

bar

hole

bar

hole

bar

During all of this, keep an eye out for schools of baitfish. Over the course of the season, bays and coves are home to many prey species, including Atlantic silversides, bay anchovies, and squid. But in the Northeast, the one that perhaps draws the most action is juvenile menhaden, often referred to as baby bunker or peanut bunker. Typically these young menhaden are easy to spot. For one thing, they school very tightly together and thereby become a large, visible mass. On calm days, you can see them from quite a distance because they feed on top, dimpling the surface like rain. Any streamer of 2 to 4 inches with plenty of flash may do the trick, but a fly that works very well is Joe Blados's Crease Fly. Adult menhaden are

When fishing a shoreline, focus your efforts where the shoreline has the most erratic shape. You'll find more bottom structure and better fishing there.

Squid are important forage items in the Northeast, especially in spring and late fall. This squid fly was tied by Chris Windram.

considerably larger, often running 12 to 16 inches in length. Wherever they pop up, you can be sure that somewhere nearby are some truly large stripers or blues. But to match this bait, you have to use a very large fly indeed.

Just as in salt ponds and lagoons a flooding tide tends to drive plankton, baitfish, and predators gradually inland, this same general pattern holds true in bays and coves as well. So it is reasonable to expect that the rear of a bay or cove will fish best during the last hours of the flood and the first of the drop. As the ebb continues, plankton, baitfish, and predators are slowly drawn toward the mouth of a bay or cove, and typically the fishing will slow at the head and improve at the mouth.

Above: *Capt. Joe Blados's Crease Fly is an excellent imitation of juvenile menhaden.* Right: *Juvenile menhaden, often called peanut or baby bunker, are one of the most important schooling baits, attracting fish from far and wide.*

The idea that fish feed more at the head of a bay during the flood and more at the mouth during the ebb has worked for me many times. Like all general rules, however, you can't expect it to hold true all the time. The most common exception to this occurs in a bay or cove that is joined by the mouth of a creek or river. These mouths typically are situated near the head of the bay or cove. As the tide starts to ebb, that causes the creek or river to begin ebbing too, and current lines and rips begin to form. This water is rich in plankton, causing forage fish, possibly in large numbers, to stack up here. As a result, the outgoing flow can hold red-hot action, which may persist all the way through to dead low tide.

Because the tide isn't forced to enter and exit through a constricted opening, these bodies of water lack the powerful, focused currents associated with an inlet. You do find areas of current, however, and these are places where fish feed. Typically the strongest currents are found at the mouth, and the faster currents and rips are apt to be at the extreme ends of the points that form the entrance to the bay or cove. Here tidal currents are fairly strong and rips are common, as water pushes by and along the point. Weaker lanes of currents are frequently associated with the sides of the bay. These areas of moving water usually are fairly broad and poorly defined, but attract fish they do. If you're lucky, you'll locate a rip or two where this lane runs over bottom structure or against an erratically shaped shoreline. In many cases, these lanes don't come within casting range of shore, and therefore they are best fished by drifting in a boat.

An angler sits at a bay mouth awaiting the tide to start moving.

Bays hold fish in all sizes. But even small bluefish are a blast if you gear down your tackle.

In some bays, the tidal currents are more or less equally distributed on both sides. There are fishing opportunities, therefore, on both sides. In other bays, things are quite different. I have encountered places where the lanes of flooding current were pretty much all on the right side of the bay, while the faster current lanes during the ebb were located on the left side. I have also been in spots where both the flood and the ebb favored the same side of a bay. Such current complexities seem common in the bays and coves of Long Island Sound and Martha's Vineyard Sound, where the general progress of the tide is oblique to the coastline. Wherever you come across these situations, you must figure them in, for where the current goes, so goes the fishing.

Fishing the Mouth of a Bay
The mouth of the bay usually has the deepest water and the fastest current, and it also receives the full force of wave and wind. Because of all that, the mouth can be a tough place to fish. Still, these waters are often home to the largest fish in the bay and are well worth the effort for that reason. On an exposed rocky shoreline, the bay's mouth may be defined by tall headlands to either side. These headlands are often steep-sided affairs with some really rough water. Out in front, waves

crash onshore, rips form, and there is apt to be a good deal of rocky bottom structure. Both wading anglers and boaters must take extra care in these places.

Because of the availability of structure and current, the mouth of a bay can
fish well at any part of the tide. Nevertheless, there are two stages of the tide I
highly recommend. The first of the incoming is often an excellent bet. As the
tide enters the bay, schools of bait hang around the mouth to feed in the flow. At
the same time, game fish that have been resting during dead low tide are now
suddenly back on the prowl. Further brightening the mix, since the water level
is low at this stage of the tide, waves are diminished and wade-fishing opportunities may exist. The second stage to consider is the final hours of the ebb. The
reasons for this are pretty much the same. During the last of the ebb, predators
and prey may drop from the head of the bay down to the mouth, and you'll
have lower water, diminished waves, and better opportunities for wading.

Try combining these two stages of the tide. Fish the end of the ebb and then
stick around for the first of the incoming. In between, you'll have about an hour
of slack tide, which is a perfect time to take a break. But if you want to continue
casting, here's an idea. At dead low, some game fish are likely to sit in deep
areas near the mouth waiting for the tide to turn. See if you can locate these resting areas. The fish in these honey holes are inactive, but because they are concentrated together, they tend to be aggressive toward an intruding fly.

If you locate a bar at that mouth, you have found a very fishy location.
These bars typically have considerable current and attract plenty of feeding fish.
Whether the bar is sand, rock, or mud, it should be productive. If a bay-mouth
bar is covered in shellfish, you have really hit the jackpot. Oyster bars are common features of protected bays along the southern Atlantic coast, and mussel
bars are numerous along the New England coast. Although these two kinds of
bars are separated geographically, both tend to form around the mouths of bays
and coves. Spotting such an oyster bar is a piece of cake: The white shells piled
up on a dark mud bottom stand out starkly. In fact, at low tide they can be seen
for a hundred yards. Mussel shells are dark, however, and the bars they form
are harder to see. But with a little observation, you'll find them too.

Shellfish like these spots because currents rich with plankton regularly sweep
by. This richness also draws other kinds of marine life, such as crabs and baitfish.
No wonder predator fish love to prowl these places. Mussel bars are home to
green crabs and silversides and attract striped bass and bluefish. Southern oyster
bars host mud crabs and mullet and draw red drum and spotted seatrout.

As good as these shellfish bars are, they present one problem: Shells can be
dangerously sharp. The shells left behind by dead oysters are not an issue, but the

shells of live oysters are. Sticking straight up from the mud, the leading edges of these shells are razor sharp. If you step on one, it could cut through your wading boot. Less dangerous but frustrating, such a shell can cut through your leader as a big fish darts for freedom.

Fishing the Middle of a Bay
No matter where you go, it's important to study the shape of the shoreline. In the midsection of a bay, be especially on the lookout for a point or bend in the shoreline; even a small one may prove to be a hotbed of angling action. Such a point or bend is likely to have associ-

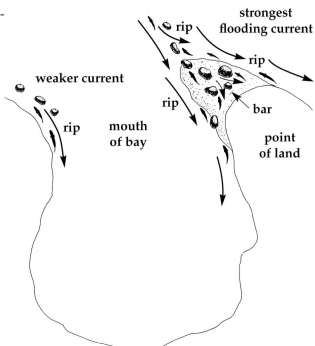

The mouth of a bay is a good place to fish, especially where strong currents exist.

Weakfish seem to like brightly colored flies, such as this Squetceiver that I tied.

ated bottom structure. It could be a bar, reef, flat, hole, or even some combination. That structure alone would draw fish, but these spots are apt to have a second attraction. Any lane of tidal current moving along this shore is going to be deflected by the bend or point. That will produce rips as well. Now you have all the ingredients for fine fishing.

As you look out over the center section of a bay, it can seem relatively featureless. Moreover, because this water may be fairly deep, discerning the presence of bottom structure can be difficult. For that reason, I highly recommend that you obtain a navigation chart of the bay. It will prove a great help in unlocking the fishing potential of these waters, as well as other portions of the bay. Look for the presence of a channel. Like the channels in salt ponds and lagoons, with their currents and depth, they supply excellent habitat for fish, especially large ones.

Also study the chart for the presence of submerged structure such as humps, reefs, and rock piles. These high spots in the bottom are popular locations for feeding fish. Keep a lookout for oyster bars and mussel bars as well. These also may be found in the middle section of a bay, and as they are at the mouth, they are very productive fishing locations. Expect predator fish to patrol the edges of submerged structure and bars where they join deeper water.

Bay and cove shorelines can be very productive. Here an angler fights a little tunny from the rocky shore of a cove.

Coves offer protected waters for those who wish to fish from light boats. This striper was caught from my drift boat.

One or more islands may be found in a bay. Like the islands in lagoons, these structures are treasure troves of angling opportunities. Currents and waves moving toward the rear are forced to move around such islands, and as they do, they create feeding lanes. The ends of islands often are connected to additional bottom structure, such as bars and drop-offs. In some cases, an island may have significant shallow flats on one or more sides. These flats might offer sight-

Weakfish love bays in the spring. Here I'm holding one from a Connecticut bay.
PHOTO BY DAVE FOLEY.

Reading a bay's bottom structure is key. Here an angler works where a dark, rocky bottom joins lighter-colored sand.

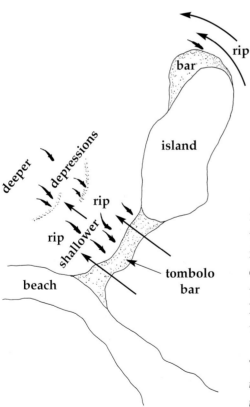

fishing opportunities, and even if not, there are fish to be caught here.

Along the Northeast coast, it is not uncommon to find an island that is connected to shore at low tide by a narrow bar. I have seen them in Pleasant Bay on Cape Cod and in Long Island Sound. These bars are called tombolos. As the tide floods and ebbs, it rushes over a tombolo and creates rip lines that draw bait and predator fish. Because the bottom is fairly shallow here, typically the best of this action happens during the last of the flood and the first of the ebb. As water levels recede, expect fish to quickly retreat back toward deeper water. With a little luck, however, you may be able to wade out from the bar and still reach them with a fly.

Tombolos are narrow bars connecting an island to the mainland. When tidal currents cross over these bars, fish come a running.

A bar connecting an island to shore is called a tombolo. When the tide rides over this bar, rips form, attracting many fish.

Fishing the Head of a Bay

Head-of-the-bay locations are very popular with anglers, and rightly so. The head of the bay typically has the best public access, a real plus in this age of no-trespassing signs, as well as a shallow, sandy shoreline. This bay-head, or pocket, beach is sheltered from most winds and overall is an easy spot to fly-fish. It may offer some of the only wading opportunities in the entire bay. And there is often a creek or river mouth at the head of a bay, a powerful magnet for fish both big and small.

To properly investigate a bay-head beach, pay a visit at low tide. A low tide around the time of either the full or new moon is your best bet, since water levels will be at their lowest. Study the surface of the water for signs of structure and current, and study the shape of the shoreline for additional clues as well. If the water level allows, wade out and familiarize yourself with the bottom structure. Also look for things that attract fish, such as eelgrass beds or shellfish bars, and see what types of baitfish are available. While you're wading, try to find where the bottom slopes away to deeper water. This edge will be a very productive place to fish during the first couple hours of the incoming tide. If the water is too deep to permit wading, don't be disappointed. Big fish like deep water. That is

Where a tidal creek enters a bay there is apt to be fine fishing.

one bonus. And it is fair to say that the fishing that deep-water beaches offer is less tide-dependent, so you can fish them confidently at any stage of the tide. If big fish are what you're after, however, the last hours of the flooding tide and the first hours of the ebb are apt to hold your best shots at memorable hookups.

In autumn, the bay-head beaches of New England are the sites of many a blitz. Striped bass and bluefish love to pin schools of bait against these shores. The blitzes often take place right at your feet and are capped with a canopy of birds. Unfortunately, this action rarely lasts for more than a day or two, as migratory fish are on the move. The best conditions for a blitz seem to occur when the higher stages of the tide arrive at dawn, particularly on days when the wind is driving straight into the bay. Hit it right, and you'll get a fish on every cast.

Check out any creek or river mouths at the head of the bay; these are likely to prove a gold mine. It's hard to overestimate their fishing potential. Often they are large and impossible to miss, but in some cases, they may flow only periodically. A salt pond inlet, for example, may open and close with the seasons. It may flow strongly in the spring when the pond is filled with rain, and then dry up in the summer. Strong moon tides can also be a factor. These tides may push across the beach and enter the pond, thereby raising its level. Later this will produce an ebbing flow.

Above: *Bays can hold some monster bluefish, and there is no more fun way to catch them than on a popper.* Right: *Bob's Banger is an excellent popper.*

The plankton that concentrates around the mouth attracts large schools of baitfish such as silversides and sand eels. Moreover, in the early spring, even a small tidal creek may host a herring run. If that is the case, this spot is going to draw plenty of attention from striped bass. One way to find out is to walk the creek banks looking for herring swimming upstream. Take your time; herring can be difficult to spot. Look at the mouth too; you may see a school preparing to enter. Even if you can't see the herring, gulls will know if they are in town. The presence of a flock of herring gulls sitting at the mouth or along the banks of the creek is a very encouraging sign.

Seasonal inlets can be little more than a trickle. In such cases, you may find it easy to cross over and fish the opposite side, but be careful; the banks of such a

In autumn, the head of a bay can hold hot fishing. Here birds mark a school of stripers that have pinned bait against the shore.

flow are apt to be steep and very soft, and you can slip down them unexpectedly. It is common for these tiny inlets to change position over time. On one visit, you may find an inlet flowing directly into the bay, and the next time, it may dogleg to the right or left. This is something to keep in mind if you plan to fish at night.

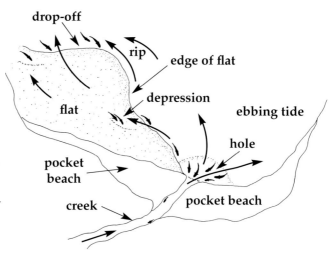

The head of a bay commonly has a creek or river mouth and extensive shallows. Expect fine fishing there.

drop-off

rip

edge of flat

depression

flat

ebbing tide

hole

pocket beach

creek

pocket beach

Never take it for granted that the flow is in a particular spot. Check before you wade through.

Study the bottom area near the mouth. Often there is important structure here and it will fish well, especially during the early hours of the ebb. Immediately outside the mouth there may be a deltalike bottom that quickly slopes away into a deep hole. That drop-off is a prime place to find fish. At the mouth, you also may find a mussel bar or an oyster bar. Should that be the case, it definitely increases your chances of success. If the bottom is sand and the creek runs hard at times, the mouth may be connected to extensive shallow structure, such as a flat or bar. All in all, the mouth makes for some fine fly rodding.

If an extensive shallow sandbar has formed, you can bet that it is well worth investigating, especially during a rising tide. The best way to learn the secrets of this bar is to do a walking tour at low tide. Pick a bright, sunny day for the venture. While holes, depressions, and trenches are certainly of interest, your primary concern is to locate any drop-offs. There should be one at the far outside edge of the bar where it joins deeper water. Watch the waves as they ride up over the flat. They'll break where the bottom first rises. This location is apt to be a red-hot destination from the last hour of the ebb until the first hours of the flood. Also be on the lookout for a drop-off along the side of the bar. While the drop-off on the outside edge is usually fairly gradual, this one could be fairly steep, quickly tapering off in deeper water or a hole. Such a drop-off not only holds fish at the low stages of the tide, but also forms a perfect travel lane for fish seeking to approach the mouth as the tide rises.

Some flats at the rear of a bay may not be adjacent to a creek mouth. Tide is still a critical factor in fishing these places, however. The most difficult time to fish is around high water. At this time, the fish can roam far and wide across the shallows in their search for food, and for that reason, they aren't concentrated. During the first half of the flood and the last half of the ebb, the fish are restricted to the deeper portions of the shallows. Here they are concentrated and more aggressive toward the fly.

If you're lucky enough to have several hours to fish a creek mouth, try this strategy: Arrive during the final two hours of the incoming tide. At this time, cast and move along the bay-head beach for 100 yards to either side of the mouth. Move slowly and cover the water well, especially where there is structure. As the tide slacks off, move to the mouth of the creek and take a break. From the beach, watch the mouth for the first signs of an ebbing current. As soon as you see it begin, move down to the water and focus all your efforts on this current.

CHAPTER 4

Fly Rodding Coastal Rivers, Tidal Creeks, and Salt Marshes

Coastal rivers, tidal creeks, and salt marshes are necessary to the health of our oceans. They are, in fact, the most essential estuaries of all. Winding in the landscape, they create a network of arteries and veins through which the life-giving richness of the land is fed to the sea. It is an intricate and beautiful system. And every time I stand by a river, I am struck by it. For without this freshwater flow, our seas could not survive.

Along the Atlantic seaboard, there are thousands of rivers, many of them legendary for their fine fishing. Starting on the Maine coast, a veritable land of rivers, some of the noteworthy ones include the Kennebec, the Saco, and the Penobscot Rivers. Moving southward into New Hampshire, there are the Piscataqua and Hampton Rivers. Massachusetts has the mighty Merrimack. In Connecticut, anglers work the Thames, the Housatonic, and the Connecticut—at 410 miles, the longest river in New England. New York has the huge Hudson, loaded with striped bass. In New Jersey, you'll find the Raritan, the Navesink, the Shrewsbury, and the Manasquan. Farther south, there are the Delaware, the Susquehanna, the Potomac, the James, the Rappahannock, and the Roanoke. And the list goes on and on.

Salt marshes and creeks are found along the entire Atlantic seaboard but are not distributed uniformly. In the New England states, a high percentage of salt marshes have been lost to development. Still, there are fair numbers in Maine, New Hampshire, and Massachusetts, but far fewer in Connecticut and Rhode Island. New Jersey seems to have a good supply, but the largest and most pristine of them are located on the South Atlantic coast, particularly in South Carolina and Georgia. Here it is possible to look out over thousands of acres of swaying marsh grass. Florida has many to offer as well, although as you move below the northern half of the state, they are gradually replaced by their tropical counterpart, mangrove swamps.

UNDERSTANDING CREEKS, SALT MARSHES, AND RIVERS

Salt marshes are coastal wetlands. They are tidal in nature and often connected to salt water via a creek. These creeks can be connected directly to the sea, but often they exit into a larger estuary, such as a cove at the lower end of a river or the head of a bay. In addition, some creeks adjoin the tide in the rear of a salt pond or lagoon. On the western shore of Barnegat Bay, for example, are Kettle Creek, Cedar Creek, Oyster Creek, Cedar Run, and Westecunk Creek, to name only a few.

From Maine to Texas, a single type of vegetation, *Spartina*, dominates creeks and marshes. Also known as saltwater cordgrass, it plays a role in your fishing there. *Spartina* grows in two forms: a short variety that forms a matted carpet on the marsh banks, and a long form that lives in the intertidal zone. The *Spartina* in the intertidal zone provides wonderful habitat for a wide range of forage, including silversides, mummichogs, killifish, crabs, amphipods, grass shrimp, and immature squid. In fact, much of the diet of the fish that inhabit these

Tidal creeks are great places for light fly rods in line weights 6 to 8.

Spartina *grass provides a holding area for plenty of bait.*

waters is found here. And because of it, predator fish frequently patrol near the edges of the flooded grass.

The forage in creeks and marshes is, for the most part, relatively small, and therefore scaled-down saltwater flies in sizes 1 through 4 are effective. Depending on what part of the Atlantic you're fishing, you could be serving those flies to bluefish, weakfish, spotted seatrout, red drum, ladyfish, or others. Many of them will be juvenile, under 2 feet in length, although occasionally a 10-pound or bigger fish spices things up. But all in all, creeks and marshes are perfect light-tackle country, where a 6-weight fly rod can often shine.

Besides being perfect for light fly rods, creeks and marshes are ideal for canoes, kayaks, and rowboats. In fact, nowhere in the salt do these craft better fit in. Wade fishing is possible, too, but usually limited. The mud bottoms are often very soft and unable to bear your full weight. So unless you don't mind being stuck knee-deep in a quagmire, proceed with caution. Fishing from shore is a viable option, and usually there is plenty of room for a backcast, though some care is required here too. The matted grass on the marsh can hide holes, and the ground can be a bit spongy, so move slowly. The banks may be undercut by waves and current, and they can suddenly slump without warning. For that reason, it's wise to stand back a few steps from the edge. In some locations, you can walk the banks only during the weaker tides of the month; on the stronger tides, they are too flooded with water.

Shrimp patterns work well in estuaries, including tidal creeks. This is Bob Popovics's Ultra Shrimp.

In the spring, river herring are the largest baitfish in many rivers and are a magnet for striped bass. These river herring range from juvenile to adult.

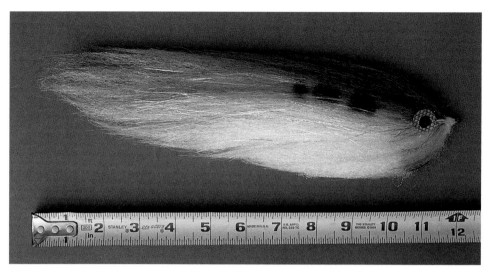

Matching adult river herring or adult menhaden requires large flies. This is Pat's Big Bunker, tied by Patrick Daigle. He used it to catch a striped bass over 40 inches.

An eel fly can produce some monster fish. This is a Harrington Eel created by Mike Harrington, tied by Bill Goeben. Unlike many other eel patterns, this one sheds water quickly, so it's easy to cast.

Compared with creeks and marshes, coastal rivers can be huge bodies of water, large enough to contain many different kinds of structure, such as islands, coves, flats, and bars. Along with this increase in size comes the need for additional tackle. The 6- and 7-weight rods that are so much fun in a creek can still be used in a river, but you should also have something that can chuck an 8- or 9-weight line. River fish are often munching on hearty fare such as American eels, adult menhaden, and river herring, which means you must be able to cast larger flies. In addition, river fish are not always schoolies. Ten-pound fish are not uncommon, and bigger fish are certainly around. Moreover, these fish could be sitting deep in fairly fast currents. No 6-weight will pull them out of there.

Like all other estuaries, rivers are subject to fluctuations in water level, temperature, and clarity. Because a river has a far larger watershed, the effects can be far more pronounced and prolonged. In the spring, periods of heavy rain or snowmelt runoff can dramatically raise the level of a river, and the river may not return to normal levels for a week or more. When a river swells rapidly, fish relocate from their usual haunts to avoid the increased current. They may elect to sit in the deepest portions of the river, they may move away from the main flow and take up temporary residence in the slow water along flooded banks, or they may drop down and just outside the mouth, waiting for the river to lower.

SALINITY AND THE SALTWATER WEDGE

The volume of fresh water found in a river makes the character of river fishing a bit distinct from that in other estuaries. Even in the mouth, where a river joins the salt its salinity can be relatively low, particularly in a river with a large freshwater discharge, and especially on an ebbing tide. As you move upstream, the salinity decreases further, until you reach a point where it disappears altogether. As the salinity lowers, it forms an invisible—yet very real—barrier for most saltwater game fish. For that reason, you can expect only limited river fishing for species such as bluefish, Atlantic bonito, and little tunny. And this fishing is usually largely restricted to the river mouth.

Nevertheless, there is a way saltwater game fish can safely move a fair way up inside a river. Salt water is heavier than fresh. So as a rising tide enters the river mouth, it tends to move upcurrent underneath the freshwater flow. This deep mass of brine is called a saltwater wedge. Saltwater game fish use this wedge as a highway to upstream feeding opportunities. These fish are often deep and out of view, yet they can surface unexpectedly. As the rising tide continues, the freshwater flow slows and then stalls. When that happens, the saltwater wedge climbs closer and closer to the surface. As it comes up, it may bring the fish it holds. For instance, bluefishing is often very good in the lower 5 miles of the Connecticut River, and many anglers assume that blues travel no farther upriver. Truth is, blues occasionally erupt 15 miles up inside the Connecticut River. And they got there courtesy of the saltwater wedge.

From an angling perspective, it's a trade-off. Though the presence of fresh water restricts some saltwater game fish, it is attractive to diadromous species, those fish capable of moving between fresh and salt. Diadromous fish include anadromous and amphidromous species. Anadromous fish, those that move into fresh water in order to spawn, make up the bulk. On the East Coast, American shad, hickory shad, striped bass, and sea-run trout are examples. Amphidromous fish, those that can cross into fresh water for only short stays, make up only 20 percent of the diadromous species. White perch are one.

RIVER CURRENTS AND TIDES

During the ebb, the tide and the river are pulling in the same direction. A flooding tide, however, pushes against the river. This push-pull does two things. First of all, it makes the ebbing currents much stronger than the flooding currents,

Rivers are home to some huge striped bass. This beast was caught one autumn evening in the lower Connecticut River.

and therefore the ebb may hold the better fishing, as it often does in an inlet. Second, it means that a flooding tide must work its way slowly upstream. On the Connecticut River, 6 miles up in Essex, high tide is roughly forty minutes later than it is at the river mouth. And in my hometown of Wethersfield, which is roughly 50 miles north of the river mouth, the tide is another four hours later. So when you want to fish long sections of river, you must plan accordingly.

As with inlets, time of tide and time of current are rarely the same, and because it is the current that produces angling opportunities, the difference between time of tide and time of current is significant to your fishing. Don't expect river currents to start, stop, and reverse in lockstep with the tide. On the lower Connecticut River, the current may flow upstream for ninety minutes after the scheduled high tide. Other rivers may have a substantially longer delay. The farther upriver you go, the later the incoming runs.

FISHING CREEKS AND SALT MARSHES

Creeks and salt marshes are easy to fly rod, and what's more, they are the perfect starting point for the freshwater fly rodder trying his or her hand at the brine. Because these waters are inland from the open coast, the surroundings not only are sheltered, but also are more familiar and less intimidating. All this can make things a lot easier on a newcomer. And if you're itching to try a canoe, a kayak, or a rowboat in the brine, nowhere will you feel more at home with your craft.

As the water in a tidal creek rises, game fish are encouraged to enter the creek in their endless search for food. How far they go is a factor of where the bait is most abundant, as well as the size of the creek itself. Some tidal creeks meander a fair distance back from the coast, and it's easy to assume that their upper reaches are too small and too far from the salt to contain any fish. But this is not always so. Freshwater-tolerant species, such as hickory shad and striped bass, are capable of swimming inland a long ways. And if they can fill their stomachs in those upper reaches, they are quite happy to do it. Don't be surprised to hear that someone is catching these fish on flies well inland, in a place you might never suspect.

As always, finding structure is an important key to finding fish. Points, coves, and bars—particularly shellfish bars—are great spots for that reason. The best locations are those that combine structure with current. Look for current where the tide moves out the mouth of a cove, around a point, or over a bar. Predators and prey will congregate in these rips, especially during the hours when the current is strongest.

Shellfish bars draw fish. This is an oyster bar at the mouth of a South Carolina tidal creek.

point

trib.

undercut bank

hole

trib.

drop-off

cove

hole

tidal creek

shellfish bars

undercut bank

With creeks and marshes, the shoreline is again the single largest edge. As the tide moves in and out, currents run along the banks, creating ideal feeding locations. As you watch the current move by the banks, look for areas where it is swift and patches of turbulence show on the surface. Get directly upcurrent of these locations, and deliver a fly in a down-and-across presentation.

One place you'll nearly always find fast current is at a bend in the creek. Here there is also apt to be a deep hole. Since creeks are shallow, any hole is a very attractive structure for game fish, especially the largest fish in the area. Expect the hole to be on the outside of the bend where the current is strongest. Also keep an eye out for holes wherever a tributary joins the creek or where two creeks come together. Once you find a hole, try a weighted fly and even a sinking fly line.

Tidal creeks are easy and fun to fish. True, the fish may be small, but you can use the lightest-weight saltwater fly rods.

Pay particular attention to any shoreline heavily rimmed in *Spartina* grass; there will be a lot of bait here. Perhaps the most common species you'll encounter is the Atlantic silversides, which usually runs anywhere from 2 to 5 inches in length. At higher stages of the tide, the bait hides in the flooded grass. Game fish prowl the edges of the grass at this time, seeking a meal. Because the bait is tight to the banks, the action is usually there too, so it pays to angle your cast parallel to the shoreline. The best action often occurs as the tide turns and starts to ebb.

Sea-run trout on the Atlantic often spawn by running up rivers and creeks in the back of a bay. (This is not referring to weakfish or spotted seatrout, both of which are sometimes called trout.) These runs frequently occur late in the year, starting in November or December, although a few runs occur in late winter and early spring. The fish stage outside the mouth, waiting for the right conditions

Above: *There are many excellent patterns to mimic silversides. Bob Veverka's Silverside is one of them.* Right: *Atlantic silversides can be found in many estuary locations and are fed upon by many fish.*

to enter. A heavy rainfall that raises the river levels often is the trigger that spurs them to move in. I have also seen the sea-runs enter a creek on a flooding November moon tide. Fishing around the mouth at these times is usually productive, and I recommend a flooding current over the ebb.

Where sea-runs are concerned, don't expect large numbers. These runs tend to be small, and the fish wild and wary. Catching one or two of them is a good day. These salty trout eat sand eels, mummichogs, and other small baits, so the same 1- to 3-inch flies you use for schoolie stripers and blues work. Given the low water temperatures at this time of year, the fish are likely close to the bottom. Try a weighted fly such as a Clouser or Jiggy. You may also need a sinking-tip fly line. Avoid heavy footsteps, walk slowly along the bank, and keep your silhouette low; these fish are spooky.

INDICATOR FISHING

Strike indicators can be a blast in tidal creeks. I use them with my 6-weight rod to catch striped bass and hickory shad, and I'm positive this tactic can take many other species as well. Where stripers are concerned, I employ the idea most often in early spring and late fall. At those times, the water is cool and the fish are less likely to chase a fast-moving fly, so the dead-drift approach is ideal.

You can certainly dead-drift a fly without an indicator, but an indicator has several advantages. It allows you to control the depth at which the fly runs and to accurately position the drift. I often cast slightly beyond the lane in which I want the fly to ride, then, by pulling with the rod, I slide the indicator over until it is in the exact spot where I want the drift to begin. That's very helpful. Last but not least, an indicator signals even the lightest bite.

Occasionally I'll rig with two flies. This permits me to fish two different patterns and work two different depths. The larger of the two is attached to the end of the leader. I then tie a 20-inch piece of tippet material to the bend of the hook. To the end of that, I attach the second fly. To help the indicator carry the weight, I coat it with conventional fly floatant, the type trout anglers use on a dry fly, and I may reapply it every half hour.

My basic strategy is simple: Either from shore or while wading, I cast upcurrent and allow the indicator to drift back toward me, mending line if necessary. Eventually the indicator passes by me and continues downstream. Once it is below me, I retrieve it back slowly, in short strips with long pauses. You can also do this from a boat, and if the boat and the indicator are moving along at the same speed, you can get a very long drift.

Because the fly has no real action, the only way the fish are aware of it is if they see it. So this tactic works best in fairly clear water. Even there I like to impart a little action to the fly; it often triggers a hard strike. A chop on the water can do it for you. The indicator bobs, and that causes the fly to jiggle as it rides downcurrent. On a calm day, however, the action is up to you. Here's how you do it: Cast upcurrent and hold the rod tip high. As the indicator comes toward you, twitch the rod, pulling on the line. Continue to occasionally twitch the indicator as the fly passes downstream of your position. Don't yank; you only want to move the indicator about 4 inches each time. Pause between twitches so the fly can swing back down under the indicator.

Indicators are a great help in serving a fly tight to a marsh bank. By standing back from the water, you can drift a fly within inches of the water's edge, and that's where the fish sometimes are. If you want a long drift, walk slowly along the shore with your rod held high, following the indicator

Hickory shad are like tiny tarpon; they jump and pull far out of proportion to their size. Tidal creeks, rivers, and bays are home to them.

downcurrent. Fish love to hold underneath a bridge, where the down-and-across presentation is difficult to use, but you can go to the downcurrent side of the bridge and cast your indicator rig underneath. Pay particular attention to the water that runs along the bridge abutments; the fish are usually sitting right there.

When you dead-drift a fly, the strikes can be very subtle. Be ready at all times, and don't expect every fish to pull the indicator under. Some fish do, but many times all you'll see is the indicator behaving oddly. It slows down; it stops for a second; it twitches a little. As soon as you see any of these things, set the hook immediately; don't wait. Failure to do so results in one of two problems:

Dead-drifting flies under a strike indicator is effective in tidal creeks. These indicators are 3/4 inch in diameter and will support a fly on a size 1 hook.

Either you'll miss the fish, or you'll inadvertently hook some fish deeply, especially with a small fly. Because of that potential problem, it's best to pinch down the barbs on your hooks. If you are consistently hooking fish deep, cut off the indicator and fish conventionally.

Small Clouser Minnows work well, as do streamers tied with white marabou. In both cases, use some flash. Also try shrimp, crab, and worm patterns. They work too. I have also hooked fish using large, weighted freshwater nymphs. The best of those have been beadhead stonefly nymphs. Sound strange? It's not. Juvenile striped bass living at the heads of estuaries eat aquatic insects much like a trout does, and the nymphs also look a little like shrimp. But I'll warn you that nymphs on freshwater bronze hooks don't like salt water. They rust.

Most of the commercially available strike indicators are designed to support small freshwater flies and consequently are of little use in the salt. There are exceptions, however. Sierra Pacific Products (www.sierrapac.com), for example, has a product called Micro Ball Indicators. The X-Large size is a 3/4-inch-diameter foam ball that can be used individually or ganged together to support a larger fly. They are convenient, reusable, and inexpensive. If you can't find a suitable indicator, shape your own out of foam, cork, or a premade popper body. In fact, you can tie a tippet off the bend of a popper and use it as your indicator. This is called a popper-dropper rig.

Just as in freshwater fishing, the distance between the indicator and the fly is determined by how deep you think the fish are holding. When you see fish grabbing bait near the surface, you can set the indicator as close as a foot or two above the fly. Where the fish are deeper, set the indicator accordingly. When searching creeks, I typically have mine anywhere from 3 to 6 feet above the fly. Now and then, I'll use two flies in order to cover two depths. The first fly is the larger of the two and is tied directly to the tippet. Then I tie an 18-inch piece of tippet to the hook bend and attach my second fly.

WORM HATCHES

Worm hatches can be found in creeks as well as salt ponds and lagoons. A mud bottom littered with broken shells provides the best habitat. These hatches are seasonal in nature, occurring mainly in the spring, although some may repeat into early summer. The exact timing of the hatch seems to vary considerably from location to location, and for that reason, local knowledge becomes extremely important.

Worm hatches in southern New England typically kick off in May. Many of these events seem to be triggered by the phase of the moon. Look for the hatches to take place over a three- or four-day period around the time of the full or new moon, although the new moon is a more likely bet. The hatch starts each day just

Worm hatches are a springtime event in many northeastern tidal creeks.

as high tide crests and the ebb begins. While they may hatch on a daytime high tide, more often the worms wait for the high tide that takes place in low light. Once the worms get going, they are apt to continue hatching all the way to dead low tide, supplying you with six hours of fishing. And the hatch may repeat in the same location, on the same moon tide, in June and possibly July.

Other hatches, particularly those that take place in salt ponds, appear to be unrelated to the phase of the moon. Instead, water temperature is the controlling factor. Look for these hatches to begin as the water reaches about 65 degrees F in the shallows. That sounds pretty warm for May, but these locations have very shallow water and dark-colored bottoms that soak up the sun. The worms come off in the light at any time of day, although the timing is, to a degree, influenced by the tides. Typically the hatch doesn't occur as the tide is flooding, probably because the flood tends to cool water temperatures down. The ebb is usually better, since it draws warmer water out from the shallows. Best of all is an ebbing tide that starts at the warmest part of the day. In a large body of water, one of these hatches may last for three weeks, moving day by day from one section to another—great fishing.

Commercially available worm flies are usually dark red. These do work, and sometimes very well, but flies tied in lighter shades bordering on pale pink can be even more deadly. In general, worm flies are tied on hooks from size 4 up to 1/0, with the overall length varying from 1 to 3 inches. The majority of these are subsurface patterns. Floating worm flies, however, are excellent producers and should be in your fly box. They can be created with foam or deer hair.

Worm hatches attract striped bass in droves.

Worm flies range from brick red to pale pink and can be tied in both subsurface and floating styles.

Because the worms swim slowly, erratically, and sometimes with a looping action, it can be difficult to make your fly behave naturally. A strike indicator can be the solution. Observe the depth at which the worms are active, and set your indicator accordingly. If there is current, dead-drift the fly through the feeding fish. If there is no current, cast out into a promising area. Let the fly settle, and then sweep the rod to your side very slowly. The idea is to cause the fly to travel a few feet back toward you. Stop, permitting the fly to rest, reel up the slack, and then sweep the rod again.

FISHING RIVERS

Rivers course over long distances, traveling through varied terrain and over varied substrate. They widen, they narrow, they twist and turn. And all the while, their gradient is changing. One place the bottom is flat as a board and the current is like glass, while just around the bend the river roars over a bottom as steep as a ski jump. As a result, rivers change mile after mile, and that is what makes river fishing so interesting.

Perhaps because of all this variety, predator fish can be very particular, congregating only in selected areas. So don't be surprised if the best angling opportunities are restricted to small sections of the river. That means you have to go find the fish. Being mobile is a help, whether you drift sections in a boat or drive to various areas of the shoreline by car. Here again, your search revolves mainly around understanding tides and currents, structure, and prey.

How far upriver do tides go? Some anglers wrongly assume that the tide is important only down near the river mouth; not so. Tides can travel up a river a very long way. Truth is, sometimes it seems the only things that stop them are dams. The tide in the Connecticut River, for instance, is felt all the way to the Enfield Dam, roughly 60 miles upstream. In the Hudson River, tidal influences reach 150 miles north to Troy. It takes time for the tide to ride up that far. In the case of the Connecticut, the tide takes roughly five hours to travel 50 miles.

As elsewhere, tides in a river affect current and depth, and those things determine where fish locate and when they feed. During the ebb, river currents are at their peak strength, and water depths are lowering. Because of these things, as the ebb progresses, fish tend to drop out of shallow areas and head for deeper bottom structure. As the currents build, expect the fish to be increasingly concentrated and tightly associated with the structure. On the flood, the picture is totally different. Water levels begin to rise, the currents reverse, and their speed tapers off. During these changes, game fish relocate, typically spreading out to feed in shallow areas.

Because the fish are concentrated during the ebb, they can be harder to find. In fact, it may seem that the river is totally devoid of life. While luck always plays a role in angling, during the ebb it's anglers who know the bottom structure who consistently do well. They understand where the fish are apt to be and can focus all their effort on those prime spots. Therefore, you must study the river. Boats equipped with electronic fish finders can be a tremendous aid, but you can learn a lot by reading navigation charts, listening to fishing reports, and being persistent.

Now for the good news. Although it may be difficult to locate fish during

Drifting along and casting to the bank is a great way to find fish in the river. This schoolie was caught from my drift boat.

the ebb, once you have found them, you have likely found a bunch. And as they're creatures of habit, they are apt to use that same holding area again and again. Furthermore, on a strong ebbing current, the fish may be willing biters. Because they are likely to be tight to the bottom structure, however, don't expect them to move up far for a fly. You'll have to deliver the goods right to them. So you'll probably need a fast-sinking line with a short leader, and perhaps a weighted fly as well. And just as important, you must cover the water slowly and methodically.

The fish are typically easier to locate during the flood tide, although you're apt to find less of them in any one location. Instead of covering the water methodically as on the ebb, now you are much better off casting and moving in an effort to intercept the fish. One place to search for fish is on flats. This is particularly true in the spring, when the warm water in the shallows is likely to attract fish. During the flood, also look up inside tributaries.

Watch for days when the right stage of the tide occurs at the right light level. Truth is, no matter what kind of estuary you're in, linking light and tide is a wise idea. Here's an example. In the Connecticut River, the striper bite usually heats up for a short time around dusk and dawn. This bite may last for only an hour, but it could well be the fastest fishing of the entire day. By examining a tide chart, you can locate days when the stage of the tide you want takes place during low-light hours. Those days are very likely to produce.

Rivers hold pretty much all the same kinds of bottom structure as other estuaries, including channels, coves, tidal creek mouths, flats, bars, and islands. And the same tactics can be used as well. Still, rivers have their own special character, including two man-made structures that often occur: bridges and dams.

Savvy river anglers know that the channel plays a significant role. For one thing, given the strong and pervasive currents in a river, the channel offers fish a chance to get out of the flow. But fish like the channel for other reasons too. Most predator fish prefer to be in the shadows, and the depths of the channel are a perfect place to avoid bright light. Those depths are also a haven from water temperature extremes; the channel is cooler in summer and warmer in late fall and winter. Moreover, predators seem to like a quiet sanctuary where they can rest and recharge their batteries. The channel supplies this as well.

Fish don't sit everywhere in the channel; they're picky. They usually gravitate to the deepest holes, and the deepest hole in a section of river is apt to be attractive not only to the most fish, but to the largest ones as well. Although deep holes may be found anywhere in a river, they are more likely in certain areas. A bend in the river is one place to investigate, and the sharper the bend, the better. The section of the river downstream of an island is another place to expect a hole, and immediately outside a tributary mouth is a third. You can locate these deep holes

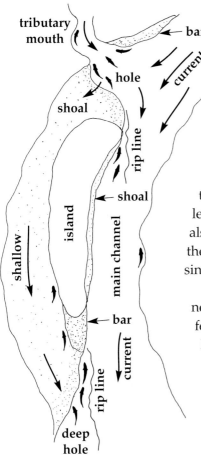

Rivers are fascinating places, but it takes time to learn their structure and currents.

by studying a navigation chart or using a depth finder. Any way you do it, it is time well spent.

Fish may be in these holes at any stage of the tide or time of day, but some conditions are more favorable. Try fishing deep holes during the final hours of the ebb; this is often a prime time for two reasons: First, as water levels drop, fish are forced to concentrate in the deep spots. Second, it is imperative to get the fly right to the bottom, and lower water levels make it easier for you to do that. Fish are also likely to be home during the brightest hours of the day, particularly if it's sunny. In all cases, fast-sinking lines and short leaders are the way to go.

The most productive deep holes are those lying near a feeding area, and one of the most important feeding areas is a cove. Coves are often much shallower than the main stem of the river. This allows them to warm up quickly in the spring, attracting predators and prey. For instance, a warm shallow cove is an ideal spot for river herring to spawn. A cove often contains a tributary mouth, which also draws predators and prey.

A deep hole immediately outside a tributary mouth is bound to produce. Currents are relatively strong here, especially on the ebb, and there is usually plenty of adjacent bottom structure as well. Anadromous fish, like striped bass and river herring, often stage in these locations before running up inside. If the tributary is too small for larger predatory fish to enter, expect them to station themselves in the hole awaiting the baitfish to exit. If the tributary is large, predators may enter on the flooding tide and run up as far as water depths allow. In the Connecticut River, it is common for striped bass to follow herring up the larger tributaries, such as the Salmon and Farmington Rivers.

If you find a deep hole situated downstream of a riffle, you may have hit pay dirt. A riffle is a section of river where the current speeds up as it goes over a shallow, uneven stretch of bottom. Riffles typically have tons of turbulence and some churning whitewater as well, and they are easy to spot. Like coves, riffles are feeding stations. Expect fish to be up in the riffle during the higher stages of the tide, and then to fall back into the hole during the final hours of the ebb. Also be on the lookout for a hole that adjoins a large flat or bar.

One more place to look is downstream of an island. Fact is, some of the finest fishing opportunities in a coastal river are found around islands. As in other estuaries, islands frequently have many favorable features, including bars, drop-offs, holes, flats, and rip currents. It is common for one side of the island to press against the main channel, while the opposite side holds shallow flats. And you may find a tributary entering above, below, or even behind the island. On the downstream end of the island, rips are common, especially on the ebb, and deep holes are frequently found nearby.

Dams

Although as a nation we are considerably wiser today about the environmental problems created by dams, too often they still deny anadromous fish an opportunity to ascend to their native spawning grounds. Dams are, nevertheless, a reality in many rivers, and they often offer fine fishing.

Currents below a dam are like the currents in the mouth of an inlet; the water is likely swift, deep, and canalized. Moreover, the best fish-holding currents and structure usually favor one side of the river. That is the side you want to be on, if access allows. A good many fish are likely sitting tight to the base of the dam, particularly where there is deep water or a back eddy. If you can safely get within range, the fishing here could be easy as shooting fish in a barrel. But before you wet a line there, read the regulations. Local fishing laws may restrict how close you're allowed to get.

In many locations, directly downstream of the dam are one or more bars running parallel to the main current. Check them out. It's quite possible that these structures permit a wading angler an excellent shot at fish, although wading here may be risky. No matter where below the dam you decide to fish, getting a fly down through the swift current is frequently a problem. Yes, occasionally fish will take a fly up top, but often that wonderful business happens only in low light. The rest of the time, if you can't deliver your goods deep, you may end up batting zero. So don't show up without a fast-sinking fly line and weighted flies; you'll likely need them.

The tailwater below a dam can be exceedingly swift and powerful—even downright dangerous. So wading or boating below a dam requires the utmost caution. Some of these dams also periodically release water, either to regulate river flow or to create hydroelectric power. When water is released, water levels

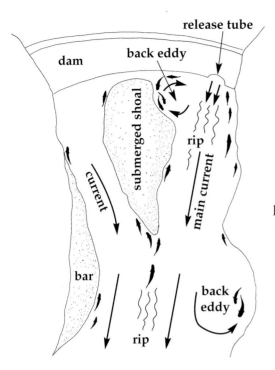

The stretch of water immediately downstream of a dam is apt to host fine fishing. But the current and turbulence can also make it a dangerous place.

below the dam may suddenly surge, producing swift currents, turbulence, and a rapid rise in the river. Downstream of the Weldon Dam on the Roanoke, for instance, the water can jump 5 feet in a single hour. This poses a very real hazard for shoreline and wading anglers, as well as those in boats. Some, but not all, dams post a schedule of releases and may have a horn announcing a pending release. If you are unaware of a particular dam's release schedule, it is always wise to ask questions in a local tackle shop. Above all, stay alert.

Bridges

For river anglers, fishing around bridges is a time-honored tradition. Here you'll find all the right ingredients: deep water, swift currents, and pronounced bottom structure. Easy public access is also common. Much of the angling centers on the bridge abutments. These are the physical supports carrying the weight of the span. Standing in the river, they deflect the current and in so doing create rip lines, seams, and back eddies, all of which fish love.

Current direction determines which side of the bridge holds more action, with the downcurrent side being the better bet. This is not to say that fish do not sit upcurrent of the bridge, but this is less typical. In order to avoid the current's forces, many of the fish are tight to the abutments. Consequently, fly placement can be critical. And a fast-sinking line is often the only way to properly deliver the fly.

Bridge fishing is often accomplished from a boat. A boat allows you not only to fish more water, but also to position yourself to cover the prime areas. That's a huge help. Bridges are often areas of heavy boat traffic, however. And you must be careful when anchoring near a bridge. In some cases, electrical and telephone transmission cable may be on the bottom. If so, signs should indicate this. It is also common to have construction rubble and bottom debris near bridges, all of which can permanently snag your anchor.

Bridges provide a lot of current and bottom structure and produce prime fishing opportunities.

Anglers on foot still get a share of the fish. In some bridge locations, a bar forms along one shoreline. These bridge bars tend to be long, narrow affairs, although I have seen a few that were wide enough to extend halfway across the river. Wade-fishing may be possible. Take care, as some river bottoms are very soft, and the outside edge of the bar may drop away suddenly into the channel. Expect the most productive area to be right along the drop-off. The fish are apt to be tight, so fly placement is important. If you can't wade the bar, take heart: You may have a shot from shore during periods of high water and low light, when fish may come up on the bar to feed.

Taut-Line Jigging

No matter where you fish in a river, strong current can make getting the fly down to the fish a real problem. These fish are very reluctant to move far for a

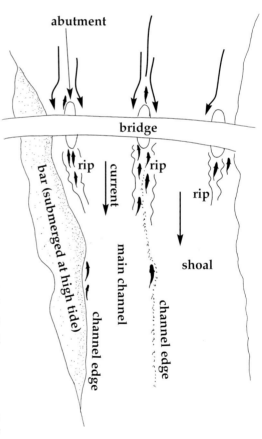

The wise river angler knows that waters near a bridge are an angling gold mine.

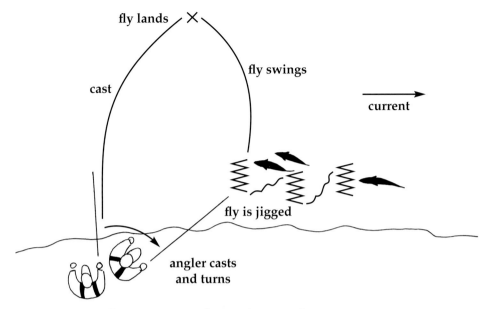

Taut-line jigging allows you to cover fast-moving water better.

fly, so it's important to present that fly close to the location where you think the fish are likely holding. But even so, the fly may swing past the fish so quickly that they have little time to react. Taut-line jigging is a trick that overcomes that problem by keeping the fly in the strike zone, and it can greatly increase your hookups.

Cast across the current, and allow the fly to swing through the area where you think the fish are holding. When the line hangs straight downcurrent, make several short strips, retrieving the fly back 3 or 4 feet. If no hookup is forthcoming, stop retrieving and allow the current to slip the line slowly through your fingers. Once the fly has returned to its original position, again strip the fly back a short distance. Repeat this operation several times, in an attempt to tease any fish into striking.

If there are no takers, pull off 6 additional feet of fly line, and allow the current to pull the fly farther downstream. Once the line comes tight, start over again. Retrieve 3 to 4 feet of line, and then allow it to be pulled downstream by the current. This tactic keeps the fly bouncing in the fish's face, provoking them to whack it. I've seen it work wonders on striped bass and American shad.

CHAPTER FIVE

Gear, Regulations, and Technique

Fishing gear—we look at it in catalogues and talk about it with our friends. How much of it you really need is open to debate. Some anglers seem to get by with very little, while other anglers own everything under the sun. Personality plays a role here, as does the size of your bank account. Regardless of what type of angler you are, however, one thing is certain: The right gear is essential, and you need to rig it correctly and know how to use it.

FLY RODS

There is no piece of tackle we depend on more than our fly rods, and there is no gear we grow more attached to. Get the right rod and you're in heaven. You feel comfortable casting it, and life on the water is a cakewalk. Pick the wrong rod—one that doesn't suit your casting style or is too light or heavy for the job at hand—and your angling adventures come unglued.

Estuary fishing is diverse. One day you might be in an inlet, gunning for big fish. To get the job done, you're chucking big flies and heavy sinking lines. Believe me, this is a game that warrants a rod with backbone. Another day you could be in a river, working over busting fish from 5 to 10 pounds with intermediate lines and 1/0 flies. Here you'll need a slightly lighter rod. On still another occasion you might be wading the shallows of a salt pond. Now you can consider an even lighter rod, one that's fun with school-size fish and can make the delicate presentations that sight fishing demands.

One size fly rod can't excel at both ends of that spectrum, not by a long shot. If any rod comes even close, it's probably a 9-foot, 8-weight. Nevertheless, it's

Given the variety of situations you encounter in estuaries, it helps to have a selection of rods.

best to have at least two different size rods, ideally three. Having a selection of rods allows you to more closely match your tackle to a variety of situations. And best of all, you can better match the rod to the size of the fish. That's the key to getting the maximum enjoyment from our sport.

For sight-fishing on the flats, and wherever the fish are running small— five pounds or less—and close to the surface, I like a 9-foot, 6-weight. Not a freshwater 6-weight, but one specifically designed for the salt. Mine is a Scott STS. It is capable of launching the entire line and easily flings flies

You need a big fly rod to lift a big fish.

up to size 2. Given the small diameter of a 6-weight fly line, these light rods make gentle presentations and turn schoolies into tigers. When 1/0 flies are required, or where the fish are chunkier and a sinking line may be needed to reach them, I prefer an 8-weight. The 8-weight has the power to handle fish to 10 pounds or more, particularly if you don't have to pull them from down deep. It's also a fine rod for working out of a boat. For the bigger inlets, for chucking flies to size 3/0, and wherever broad-shouldered fish hang in swift, deep currents, I want my 10-weight. It hurls the extra-fast-sinking fly lines needed to hit pay dirt, and it can pump those big, bad boys out of the briny depths.

In terms of rod length, I suggest a 9-footer. Anglers who regularly fish from canoes or kayaks often opt for a slightly longer rod in the hopes it will help keep their backcasts off the water. I understand that concern, but I strongly believe that the answer to that problem lies in learning to properly cast in the first place. Keep your backcasts high.

Two-piece rods are the most popular, but three-, four-, and even five-piece rods are gaining favor. Today's multipiece rods are far superior to those offered years ago. These rods cast just as well as two-piece rods and are only slightly heavier. A multipiece rod packs down into a shorter tube and is therefore easier to transport, not just in cars and planes; if you're fishing from a small boat, you'll reap the benefit too.

Look a fly rod over carefully before you select it. It should be saltwater-ready with a fighting butt, oversize guides, and corrosion-resistant hardware. The rod should also have a full-wells style grip. Check to see that it fits your hand. A grip that is too big for your hand is going to be tiring, and a grip that is too short will be uncomfortable. Check the quality of the rod's grip as well; it's a good indication of the care that went into making the rod. Individual cork rings fitted onto the rod blank make the best cork grips. This is a time-consuming process, but it creates a stronger, long-lasting grip. For cost reasons, however, manufacturers may use premade grips and then simply adapt them to a rod. Because the individual rings were not hand-fitted to the blank, there may be voids between a premade grip and the rod blank. Over time, these voids will cause the cork rings to separate or crack. Squeeze the grip along its entire length; there should be no really soft spots.

The most mysterious aspect of selecting a rod is picking the right action. For one thing, rod action is hard to precisely quantify and a bit subjective. What one manufacturer may call fast action, another may deem moderately fast. Adding to the confusion, you'll hear different opinions as to what constitutes the best rod action. One way through this maze is to seek professional advice from a fly-fishing shop staffed by experienced saltwater anglers. Here are some things to consider.

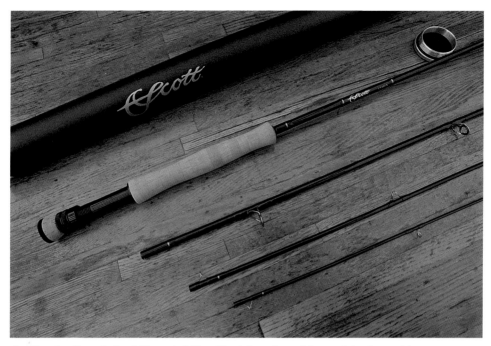

A saltwater fly rod should have a full-wells style grip and large stripping guides.

Many manufacturers have several different models in their lineups, each with its own type of action. These models cover a pretty wide gamut, from rods described as fast or ultrafast to others called moderately fast to others slower still, perhaps called progressive action. The fastest-action rods are frequently touted as the state-of-the art tools for the brine. In fact, some folks profess that these rods are the only type saltwater anglers should consider. Granted, ultrafast rods generate high line speeds, which means they are capable of long, accurate casts. They are also excellent in windy conditions. All of that is helpful, no question. The fastest-action rods are, however, not right for everyone.

An extremely fast-action rod can really shine in the hands of a highly experienced caster, particularly one of above-average size and strength. But the average caster often finds such a rod difficult to use and even downright uncomfortable. A moderately fast-action rod, on the other hand, still generates excellent line speed and throws good, long casts, but its slightly slower action makes it friendlier to cast, and it requires less physical energy to use. In short, it's a better rod for the majority of anglers. Progressive-action rods are super rods for working with fine tippets, and they make very soft presentations, which can be helpful when sight-fishing. They're best for short-range work in relatively calm conditions.

When it comes to rod action, the important thing is how well you can cast with the rod. If the fly shop has a rental or loaner rod of the type you're interested in, fish a day with it to see how it handles. If not, cast with a few demo rods at the shop. I prefer to take along my own fly lines for this job; it cuts down on the variables. If you are going to use the shop's lines, ask the salesperson what kind of line it is. If you're used to casting lines with 40-foot tapers, a 27-foot taper is going to feel mighty odd, and you don't want to blame the rod for it. Nor can you expect a floating line to cast as far as an intermediate. Demo lines frequently have been sitting on a reel for eons, so they may come off in coils and may be pretty beat. Stretch the line, and have something along to clean it with. If you want to evaluate rods fairly, it's important to take this kind of care.

Most important, learn to cast properly. No rod can solve your casting problems; that's up to you. Practice is part of the equation; lessons, books, and videos can aid as well. Yes, sometimes the fish are right at your feet, but the ability to throw a long line not only allows you to cover more water, but also provides the required stealth where fishing pressure is heavy and fish are spooky. And where fish are very deep, a long cast delivers more sinking line to the water, and that assists in taking your fly to the strike zone. Learning to cast well is worth the effort.

REELS

This may be the golden age of saltwater fly reels; there are loads of them on the market. Most are saltwater ready and have smooth, consistent drags capable of taking on the power of saltwater species. They are available in a wide price range, from expensive, top-of-the-line beauties to serviceable reels at moderate rates. You can expect to find something for just about any budget. That's good news.

In picking a reel, size matters. The reel you purchase must have sufficient capacity to hold your fly line and an adequate amount of backing. How much is adequate? That depends, for one thing, on how good an angler you are. In the estuaries of the Northeast, an experienced fly rodder can stop just about anything with fins in 65 to 75 yards. An inexperienced angler, on the other hand, might allow some of those fish to go twice that distance. But skill aside, here are some basic guidelines.

If you're fishing primarily in shallow water for striped bass, bluefish, red drum, hickory shad, spotted seatrout, or weakfish less than 10 pounds, it's very rare to need more than 100 yards of 20-pound backing. To be on the safe side, however, let's say 150 yards. But if a reel is to be used primarily for larger fish, particularly for speed demons such as little tunny, then 150 yards is the minimum amount required, and 200 yards of 20- or 30-pound backing gives you a comfortable cushion.

Throughout, remember two things. First, the amount of backing you can put on any reel is affected not only by the size of your fly line, but by the length, taper, and type as well. A 110-foot fly line takes up more space on your reel than a 90-foot line, and a floating line takes up more room than a sinking line, thus reducing the amount of backing the reel can store. Second, never overfill a reel. When all the fly line is loaded on the reel, there should still be enough room to squeeze a pencil between the fly line and the reel frame. Since it's nearly impossible to put the line perfectly back on the reel while fighting a fish, you'll need this extra space. Without it, the reel is apt to jam tight just as your prize draws near.

After determining the right size for your needs, you must decide whether you want a direct-drive or antireverse reel. The handle on a direct-drive turns as a fish takes line off the spool. When you're hooked to a fast-running fish, unless you get your hand out of the way, you can expect a good, sharp rap on the knuckles. Antireverse reels avoid that problem by permitting the handle to remain stationary as the fish runs, but there is a downside. When fighting a big fish, it can be hard to gain line with an antireverse reel. Every time you turn the handle, the spool can slip against the drag. It can be very frustrating. For that

Too much backing is as much of a problem as too little. Be sure that with all the line on the reel, you can still fit a pencil between the line and the reel frame.

Reels come in two types: direct-drive and antireverse. Direct-drive reels, such as the one on the right, are by far the more popular.

reason, most anglers go with a direct-drive reel and simply learn when to keep their hands out of the way. It's not hard to do.

Beyond those requirements, there are other features to consider. Large-arbor reels give you a noticeable gain in line retrieval speed and are increasingly popular for that reason. Another feature I like is a reel with a quick-release spool. During the course of a day's fishing, I may change back and forth several times between intermediate and fast-sinking lines. A quick-release spool allows me to do that smoothly and without fear of dropping screws and loose parts. I also like reels that click as line exits the spool. The noise it makes is part of the fun.

FLY LINES

At the moment, there are more fly lines on the market than I can ever remember. In part, it's because there simply are more fly-line companies. To an even larger degree, however, the increase in fly lines is attributable to advances in technology and the growing desire to create specialized lines for specific fishing situations. As a result, you can expect to see saltwater fly lines in a wide array of tapers, sink rates, lengths, and coatings, as well as those formulated for use in cold and warm climates.

Sliders are fun to fish and deadly. This slider was made by Mark Lewchik.

I'm a fan of weight-forward fly lines, constructed with the standard 40-foot taper. Fly lines with shorter tapers do permit shorter backcasts, and in some locations that is useful. They are also good for firing off quick casts, which can be helpful in working fast-moving fish such as little tunny. On the downside, a short-taper line must be retrieved farther back before you can pick up the line to make another cast; I find that inconvenient. Furthermore, the longer taper makes for a smoother-casting line, particularly for anglers new to the salt, and these lines work better with large flies.

Floating lines are the right choice when using surface flies such as poppers and sliders. And believe me, there are times when a popper or a slider is not only the most exciting fly, but the most productive one as well. It is certainly true with bass and blues; even with little tunny, some days a small slider on a floating line is absolutely deadly. Floaters are also very useful with any fly in skinny water—depths of 6 feet or less. Floating lines are also right at home on the flats, where sight-fishing situations occur in very shallow water, and because the line lies on top of the water, it helps sight-fishing anglers track the position of the fly. Floating line can be used with streamers wherever fish are feeding close to the surface.

For estuary fishing, the most versatile fly line is an intermediate. These lines sink slowly—about 1 or 2 inches a second. If you begin the retrieve immediately after the line lands, you can work your fly near the surface. If you give the line time to sink, you can reach deeper fish. Of the intermediates on the market, I prefer the clear ones, which I feel are one of the finest fly-line innovations. They shoot very well and offer an added degree of stealth. When using one, I regularly shorten my leader down to 6 feet.

Some anglers are skeptical about these clear lines, but their effectiveness was proven to me firsthand. One day a friend and I were fishing from a boat on a waist-deep flat loaded with striped bass. My friend was using a light-colored, opaque intermediate fly line, and I was using a clear one. He was retrieving a cast when a group of striped bass suddenly appeared very close to the boat, approaching his fly line at a right angle. Standing high in the boat, I saw the school stop cold upon reaching the submerged fly line. And then, rather than swim under the line, they did an about-face and swam off. No doubt they saw the fly line, and no doubt they were unhappy with it. Later in the day, I deliberately laid a clear intermediate line across the path of oncoming bass. The bass simply swam under it without even slowing down.

Though clear intermediate lines are better, they aren't perfect. They can be slick and difficult to grasp. That slickness may also preclude the use of a nail knot. If this is the case, the instructions from the manufacturer will warn you. A clear line can't be seen well during the cast, and that may cause a problem for inexperienced casters. To remedy this, grasp the front end of the fly line between two fingers, and then work along until you feel the belly taper down into the running portion of the fly line. With a black permanent laundry marker, heavily color a foot or more of the line at this juncture. So marked, you'll be able to see where the belly of the line begins. This not only will improve your casting, but also will aid you in knowing when you can pick the line up off the water.

Fly rodders love to see fish feeding on the surface, but if the fish aren't on top, never assume they're not around. In many situations—especially those

Clear intermediate fly lines cast well and provide an added measure of stealth.

involving current—fish prefer to stay deep. In fact, fish sitting on the bottom in a current often refuse every fly that you swing over their heads. Get the same fly to their depth, and voila—instantly these fish are biters. I have seen it happen often. Fast-sinking fly lines are, therefore, an essential part of your arsenal. You can't properly fish inlets or channels without them.

There are plenty of fast-sinking lines available, and they come in a variety of sink rates. If you already own an intermediate fly line, it's often best to buy a line that sinks considerably faster. I recommend the fastest-sinking line you can get. Such lines sink at rates of 4 to 6 inches a second, and they really get the fly down to those fish hiding deep.

Full-length sinking lines are quite effective, although they tend to have one problem: The entire fly line doesn't sink at the same rate, and for that reason, they tend to form a belly as they descend. That translates into slack between you and the fly—not a good thing. There are, however, some sinking lines called uniform sinks. These lines are designed to sink in a straight line, which means you can better feel the fly and better set the hook. I prefer them.

Many sinking lines, such as the popular Teeny models, are basically shooting taper designs. They have a heavy front portion connected to a long, thin running line. Often this type of sinking line is not marked in a specific line weight, but in grains. To match it up to your rod, pick one that overloads the rod but is still manageable to cast. For example, on my 10-weight rod, I use a 450-grain sinking line, even though the first 30 feet of a 10-weight fly line should weigh in at about 280 grains. Likewise, you might overload an 8-weight fly rod with a 300-grain line, or a 7-weight with a 200-grain line.

These heavy shooting taper lines can be a bear to cast, especially for the uninitiated. Don't attempt to false-cast them. With a shooting taper, you permit no more than the head and perhaps a foot or two of running line to exit the tip-top during the backcast. It's easy to see when you have it right, because the head and the running line are color coded. On the forward cast, shoot all the additional running line you possibly can, without false-casting. Since the rod is overloaded, you must also slow your casting stroke; make it more of a lob. Pinch the barb down on the fly. Above all, practice.

LEADERS

Freshwater leaders are an art form, but saltwater leaders are simpler affairs. A saltwater leader is, generally speaking, no longer than the rod and is made of no more than three sections of monofilament. For example a 9-foot leader might consist of a 4-foot butt section, a 3-foot midsection, and a 2-foot tippet. The butt section connects to the midsection with a blood knot, and the midsection to the tippet with two surgeon's loops. Easy. And if you want it easier still, there are plenty of good-quality knotless saltwater leaders available in fly shops.

The thickness of the leader butt is determined by the size of the fly line to which it is attached. For instance, when working with a 9- or 10-weight fly line, I use a butt section of 40- or possibly 50-pound-test; with a 7- or 8-weight fly line, I use 30-pound-test; and with a 6-weight, I use 25-pound-test. The midsection of the leader is constructed of monofilament one size smaller than the butt section. So with a 9- or 10-weight fly line, the midsection is 30-pound-test; with a 7- or 8-weight, it's 20-pound-test; and with a 6-weight, it's 20- or 15-pound-test. The tippet is the weakest section of the leader, and it's one size smaller than the midsection. So for the three sizes in consideration here, the tippets would be 15-, 12-, and 10-pound-test, respectively.

Having said that, there are times when shorter leaders are very useful. I regularly use leaders of 4 or 6 feet in several situations. A short leader is my standard with a fast-sinking fly line, as a long leader allows the fly to ride upward, negating the effect of the sinking line. Moreover, the arc created by a long leader hinders your ability to feel the strike. I also use short leaders at night. After all, fish are not leader-shy in the dark, and a short leader gives you a better feel for

My leader kit holds monofilament in a wide range of sizes.

the fly and produces fewer tangles. And I use shorter leaders with clear intermediate fly lines for an extra measure of stealth. On occasion, a short leader and a clear intermediate line can be a potent combo for sight fishing. Sometimes fish pop up out of nowhere, and you're forced to cast to a fish that is less than 20 feet away. At that distance, a short leader is more accurate and easier to control with so little fly line out of the rod tip.

Given the minimal length involved, these leaders can be constructed with only two sections of monofilament. Using an 8-weight fly line as an example, you might build the leader butt with 3 feet of 20-pound-test, and then attach a 2-foot, 12-pound-test tippet via loop-to-loop connections. Occasionally I even go so far as to use a leader made from a single section of monofilament.

When hunting for toothy critters such as bluefish or Spanish mackerel, you should have a shock tippet or bite tippet. A short section of 50-pound-test monofilament may do the trick; pick an abrasion-resistant brand. Using a surgeon's knot, attach the heavy monofilament to the tippet, and then attach the fly to the other end with a three-and-a-half-turn clinch knot. If you prefer a loop connection, I recommend the nonslip mono loop knot. It does a good job, although with heavy mono, you shouldn't make more than three or four turns.

Sharp teeth can slice right through even heavy monofilament, so with a mono bite tippet, you may still get cut off from time to time. I hate the idea of a fish swimming off with a fly dangling from its mouth, so I prefer using a wire bite tippet. Tobacco-colored, solid number 6 wire is the old standby. It's cheap, but it's a nuisance to work with. You have to attach it with a haywire twist, and the wire eventually kinks, making the fly track poorly. Recently a new generation of braided stainless steel wire is taking over this job. It's flexible, and best of all, it can be quickly knotted to the fly and the leader, although I caution you to make your knots carefully. Because it is braided, this type of wire may weaken after several fish, so check it for frays and replace when needed.

This new wire is sold under two brand names—Tyger Leader and Surflon Micro Supreme—and is available in a range of breaking strengths. For flies 1/0 and larger, the 30-pound-test seems a good match; with smaller flies, I use 26-pound-test. It's less bulky, and so far I have had pretty good luck with it. Apparently it isn't very obtrusive either. Recently I was using this lighter wire while fishing for blues, when a good-size little tunny socked the fly. Because these two fish mix together at times, this wire should prove mighty handy. Use a surgeon's knot (not a surgeon's loop) to connect this wire to the leader. Draw this knot down slowly and carefully, or it will not seat properly. Give it a tug to make sure it is properly set. Then attach the fly using a nonslip mono loop knot. You can connect the fly using a clinch knot, but the wire tends to curl as the knot

A new generation of flexible stainless steel wire is available for making bite tippets.

is tightened. The loop you form at the fly should be relatively small, about half an inch long. A large loop can cause trouble. The hook point may foul in it, and I have seen a large loop jump over the dumbbell eye of a Clouser, causing the fly to track improperly.

When building your own leaders, build them entirely out of one brand of monofilament. Different brands of mono have different knotting characteristics. If you knot two brands together, test the resulting leader with a spring scale before heading to the water. If the knots hold, fine. If the leader snaps well below the strength of the weakest material, you cannot use the two brands together. This same problem can occur with knotless leaders too. When the leader is worn, lengthen it by attaching some additional mono, but if the tippet material is not made of the same material, it may give you trouble. When in doubt, join the new section to the old with a loop-to-loop connection rather than a blood knot.

Fluorocarbon leader material is increasingly popular. It's touted as more invisible underwater than conventional monofilament, although I can't see any real difference. It does sink faster than monofilament, however, and is highly abrasion resistant. That toughness makes it a good candidate where sharp obstacles such as pilings or rocks present a problem. It can also be used as a shock tippet. But make your knots very carefully, as some fluorocarbon doesn't seem to hold knots very well. Never attach fluorocarbon to other leader materials without testing the strength of the resulting knot. When in doubt, always attach dissimilar materials with a loop-to-loop connection.

FLIES

Estuaries hold forage for fish in a range of sizes. So conceivably your fly box could contain quite a number of patterns, from large ones to match full-size herring on down to tiny grass shrimp flies. All of these saltwater flies fall into one of two groups: subsurface or surface.

Subsurface Flies

Subsurface flies are more prevalent and arguably more consistently productive than surface flies. They are generally tied in both weighted and unweighted versions, in sizes from 2 to 8 inches in length. The bulk of these flies are intended to match baitfish. They frequently resemble streamers or bucktail flies in construction, but many employ modern materials such as epoxy or Mylar. There are also subsurface flies to mimic other forms of marine life, such as crabs, shrimp, and worms.

When starting out, don't select flies too big for your rod to cast. Six-weight rods handle flies up to size 1; 8-weight rods are fine with flies up to size 1/0; anything bigger is best on a 9-weight or larger rod. Weighted flies such as Clouser Deep Minnows are very effective but can be trouble for novice casters. They end up whacking the rod with the fly and thereby weakening it, or worse yet, they whack themselves or bystanders. Instead, focus on unweighted streamers, and in that department, I highly recommend getting some Lefty's Deceivers. I use them extensively in hook sizes 1 to 3/0. A good alternative is any of Joe Brooks's Blonde series; they are oldies but goodies. As far as color is concerned, I'm partial to white flies, although where the water is discolored I prefer chartreuse, and at night I often use black.

Large streamers have their time and place. When gunning for big fish in an inlet, channel, or river, I carry Deceivers of 6 to 8 inches. And in a few situations, even longer streamer flies—upward of 10 inches to a foot—are best. A good example is when targeting big striped bass, which are focused on alewives in early spring and adult menhaden from summer into late fall. To match these baits, you need a lot of fly-tying material draped on the hook. You need to be a good caster and have a big fly rod to throw these creations.

Aquatic vegetation can quickly foul a fly, but it's not a problem if you have some weedless patterns. Deceivers can be tied with a weed guard of monofila-

Deceivers are a great general-purpose pattern. 3- to 4-inch ones on size 1 to 1/0 hooks are effective in many situations. These 7-inch-long, 3/0 Deceivers are for big fish such as you find in inlets.

ment or wire, but anglers in need of weed protection often use other patterns. Flies tied on keel hooks are longtime favorites in this regard. Another time-honored fly to consider is the bend-back. Both have their place in estuaries.

As your casting improves, add some weighted flies to your box. And you can't go wrong with Clouser Deep Minnows or Bob Popovics's Jiggy. For an 8-weight or larger rod, I suggest these flies in sizes 1 and 1/0 and the same colors as mentioned above. For flats work with a 6-weight rod, I use what I refer to as a Micro-Clouser. These are 1.5-inch-long Clousers tied on either a size 2 or 4 Mustad 34007. This fly requires a very small dumbbell eye; 1/36 ounce works for me. I pick subtle earth tones: tans, faded yellows, and light olives.

You may at times need a weighted fly with a full-looking profile. For those occasions, try a Half & Half. This is a Deceiver with Clouser-like dumbbell eyes at the head. It is an excellent pattern. I have used it on a hook as large as 2/0, with six long saddle hackles. You need a 10-weight rod to deliver that puppy. I also tie them long and very slender for use in matching sand eels on the flats. With two narrow hackles on small hooks, they can be made upward of 3 inches in length and still be cast on a very light fly rod.

Weighted flies may be harder to cast but are very effective. These are Bob Popovics's Jiggies.

"Niantic" Bob Hughes's PBCR is deadly on many species, including little tunny. This example was tied by Mark Koos on a circle hook.

Bob Veverka's Lazer-Tinker Mackerel is an example of how modern materials are making excellent new fly patterns.

Flies tied on circle hooks are increasingly popular. Circle hooks hold very well, but you may have to adjust how you set the hook. Often it's best to let the fish turn with the fly before you drive the steel home; in essence, you're letting the fish almost hook itself as the line tightens. Nevertheless, I know many anglers who don't wait and still seem to hook up. Overall, I think circle hooks are most effective on aggressive fish. Where and when fish are picky eaters, I feel a conventional hook does a better job.

Increasingly fly tiers are turning out subsurface patterns tied with a wide variety of synthetic materials. Epoxy flies are one example. They are durable, realistic looking, and catch a lot of fish. Perhaps the best-known epoxy fly is Bob Popovics's Surf Candy. But there are also excellent flies made with silicone, synthetic braid, and even holographic flash materials. After you have put together a selection of conventional saltwater patterns, I strongly urge you to investigate these flies made with modern materials. They're going to work for you.

Surface Flies

Surface flies come in two basic types: poppers and sliders. Poppers are slightly more aerodynamic than a cinder block; even fairly experienced anglers have trouble casting them at times. Therefore, I suggest that novice casters avoid poppers at first. It is important to choose a fly that is the right size for your rod. Try the same hook size–to–rod weight relationships given for subsurface flies. These should get you in the ballpark.

Poppers are a thrill. When a big fish pounds one, it's an unforgettable sight. Poppers require more angling skill to operate successfully, however, than just about any other fly. You must get them to pop loudly enough to attract fish, yet the speed of the retrieve can also be critical. Some fish, such as bluefish, like their poppers on the run; others, like striped bass, prefer a slower, stop-and-go style. Even after enticing a fish to nail your popper, hooking up requires additional skill. With striped bass, for example, it's best to delay the strike for a split second until the fish starts to descend with the fly. With blues, it's better to strike immediately. Your hooking success is also a factor of popper size. Large, 2/0 poppers are going to prove very frustrating with fish less than five pounds. Sure, they'll wallop the fly, but you'll miss most of them.

Sliders may not produce the spectacular strikes associated with poppers, but you're going to like them—they are exciting to use and are effective in a wider range of situations. Moreover, they are easier to cast, easier to use, and better at getting a solid hookup. I'm surprised that sliders aren't more popular; they're real fish getters. Sliders work well in calm water but are particularly deadly when presented down and across in a current. Any time of day is slider time—noon, dusk, dawn, and right through the night. Low-light conditions are prime, however, as are foggy conditions.

WADERS

On the steamy coast of the South Atlantic, some anglers wade in sneakers and shorts, particularly where clear water and sandy bottoms prevail. I think that's courting trouble, however; there are simply too many things out there that can cut or sting you. At the very least, you should wear long pants and sturdy wading shoes.

Farther north, cooler waters make chest waders mandatory. Boot-foot chest waders, with the boots permanently attached to the legs, are the way to go, and I suggest wearing a wading belt with them. Stocking-foot waders are inconvenient in the salt. The sand gets into the shoes and quickly abrades the wader feet, and the salt may corrode the eyelets on the boots, causing them to cut through the laces. Anglers who climb in and out of canoes enjoy the mobility of hip boots, which are also cheaper and cooler than conventional chest waders. You can use them pretty much any place where you can fish effectively from knee-deep water. But overall, hip boots are limited.

Choose the soles of the boots carefully. Rubber cleats are fine in sand and mud but plain dangerous on rocks, especially those coated with algae. If your part of the coast is rocky, felt soles will hold to a degree, but felt soles with metal cleats are even better. If you are a confirmed rock hopper or jetty jockey, you'll want all the traction you can get. In that case, metal cleats that slip like sandals over the soles of your boots are the best.

All waders once were made out of pretty much the same stuff, but a trip to the tackle store today reveals several materials in use. The new generation of breathable waders is the most comfortable and perhaps the best all around. The high-tech fabrics permit perspiration to exit while keeping water out. Hence, gone is the sweaty, clammy feeling once so common to life in waders. With breathable waders, salt may get into the pores of the fabric, so you should rinse them after each use.

OTHER GEAR

Pliers

Don't leave home without pliers. You'll need them to pinch down barbs, cut wire for shock tippets, and remove hooks from fish. If the fish are toothy types, you'll be able to keep your hands out of danger. Common household pliers will rust quickly, so look for ones that can stand up to the rigors of the salt. Spring-loaded ones are the best type. And get pliers that have quality cutters, capable of handling both monofilament and wire.

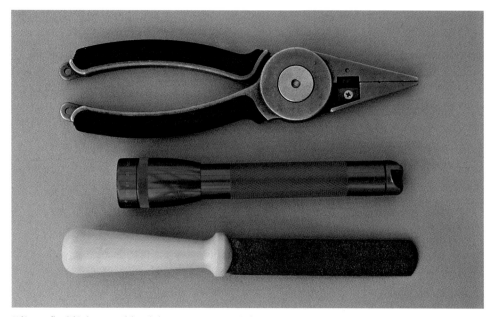

Pliers, flashlights, and hook hones are essential gear.

Flashlight
If you want to fish in low light, you'll need a flashlight. Don't scrimp here; you'll regret it one dark, lonely night. Find a light that is waterproof and durable. A focusing beam is also handy, allowing you to confine the light to the area where you need it most. Some disposable lights can be used, but pick one you trust to work. It's a good idea to carry a spare set of batteries and a spare bulb. But an even better idea is to simply carry a second light.

Hook hone
Have a hook hone with you at all times. There are plenty of them on the market. Pick one that is easy to carry and can take on even big cadmium hooks. Practice with your hone so you become fast and proficient with it. You'll grab and hold more fish if you are.

Fly boxes
Plastic fly boxes with good, corrosion-resistant hinges are the way to go. They are not pricey and hold up very well. Buy a size that not only will hold the length of flies you want to carry, but also will fit into your vest or chest pack. If you want to carry a few long flies, make sure they will fit. Buy a couple of fly boxes and load them up in ways that will make your angling easier. For instance, you may have one box solely for big flies and one solely for small. Or one box for sight fishing and another for night work. You decide.

Stripping basket
Ninety percent of the time, I use a stripping basket. You should too. It need not be fancy; a dishpan and a bungee cord do the trick. Sure, some anglers drop their fly lines in the water, on the bank, on the beach, or on the floor of the boat. But they wind up getting into trouble. In short order, the line is wrapped around something, pulled off by the current, or covered with seaweed or sand. Place that line in the basket and it's safe and sound, ready to cast. That translates into quicker and longer casts, which translates into more fish.

Polarized sunglasses
Polarized sunglasses are an important part of your gear. Granted, they are more expensive than plain sunglasses, but they work, and you really can't sight-fish without them. Gray-colored lenses are all right, but if you want to really see into the water, amber or brown is much better, especially over sandy bottoms.

Estuaries are home to mosquitoes and ticks, so take along bug repellent.

PFD

If you're a nonswimmer, you should wear a personal flotation device (PFD) whenever near deep water. Suspender-type PFDs are very popular. They are convenient, lightweight, and interfere little with casting. Some of these PFDs are activated manually with a ripcord; others self-inflate as soon as the unit gets wet. PFDs are covered in more detail in the next chapter.

Lotions and sprays

During the warmer months, take bug repellent and sunscreen with you. We have all heard the concerns over the harmful effects of the sun. Enough said. Buy some suntan lotion and use it. Mosquito bites are a growing concern, with the spread of eastern equine encephalitis and West Nile virus. Bug dope with DEET is best, but be aware that DEET will ruin many items, particularly plastics. Don't get DEET on your fly line, leader, or rod and reel. Apply the DEET to a handkerchief, and then use the handkerchief to apply it to your skin. Don't just pour DEET into the palm of your hand; it will end up on everything you touch. Aerosol sprays and roll-ons are great for this reason. Ticks also are a problem in some salt marshes. Check yourself carefully to avoid a bite.

FISHING REGULATIONS AND LICENSES

Fishing regulations change like the wind. So don't expect last year's size and bag limits to be valid this season; you must keep up-to-date on the current rules affecting your home waters. Further complicating matters, the regulations protecting a particular species may vary considerably from state to state. This is particularly true with heavily targeted game fish like striped bass, but it also can apply to smaller species you might not think of. For example, Maryland has a moratorium on the harvest of hickory shad. So if you're planning a fishing trip

Read the regulations; know the size and creel limits as well as the season. Also check to see if you need a saltwater license or possibly even a freshwater one.

out of state, check the fishing regulations at your destination. If you will be fishing from a boat and will cross the boundary between two states during a day on the water, check the regulations for both states.

State fishing regulations are printed annually in booklet form, but there are other ways to get the information. Today many state agencies, including fish and game departments, have websites, and with a few clicks of the mouse, you can download the latest regulations. You may find fishing regulations posted around boat ramps and at tackle shops, but beware—all too often these signs are out-of-date.

Also check to see if the state requires a saltwater fishing license. A small percentage of coastal states do, although if you're fishing with a licensed guide, he may possess a license valid for any angler aboard. States with saltwater licenses may also require you to purchase a special stamp or tag for some species, such as snook or tarpon.

When fishing inside some estuaries, particularly rivers, you may need a freshwater license as well. Where this is the case, well-known landmarks such as bridges typically are used to mark the boundary between fresh and salt. Size and bag limits for a species also may change as you enter fresh water. A state may have different regulations, for example, for striped bass caught in coastal waters and those caught inland in rivers.

RETRIEVE STYLES AND SPEEDS

Retrieving a fly involves imparting both speed and action. And that is what brings a fly to life. Do your job well and fish come running; do it poorly and even the right fly may not get a strike. No single retrieve style or speed works well all the time. You need to be flexible to meet various situations. When you retrieve, it's imperative to keep the rod tip as low to the water as possible, or there will be slack in the line.

There are two common methods of retrieving a fly. One involves stripping the fly back in a series of pulls and pauses; this is often called the one-handed strip. As a result, the fly surges ahead, stops, and then surges again. This method can work anytime, but it is particularly effective for flats fishing and whenever fish are less aggressive, such as when fishing for striped bass in cold water. It is the preferred method for working a popper. The other method is known as the two-handed strip, although I often call it the hand-over-hand retrieve. This can be used to move the fly in a steady, continuous motion, making it ideal for streamers and sliders. It permits a very slow retrieve, but if needed, it also can be used to produce an extremely high-speed retrieve. Because you are in constant contact with the fly, this retrieve tends to allow you to be more sensitive to the strike and therefore get a better hook set. All in all, it's the method I use more often.

Here's how to do the one-handed strip: Cast the fly out. After it lands, place the index finger of the rod hand around the fly line, and pinch it snug to the cork grip. If need be, allow time for the fly to settle down in the water column until it is at the proper depth. When you are ready, grasp the fly line immediately below the cork grip with your free hand, and then pull down a section of line until you feel tight to the fly. This is very important; if you're not tight to the fly, you'll miss many fish. While you're pulling down on the line, maintain some tension on the line with the index finger of the rod hand.

Now you're ready to start the retrieve. Release the line, pause for a second, and then reach back up to pull down another section of line. How much line you should pull in with each strip depends on water and light conditions, as well as how aggressive the fish are. There are two useful retrieve speeds to start with—slow and moderately fast. In low light or stained water, try short strips of 5 to 6 inches, with a pause of roughly a second long between them. This slow retrieve is also useful when fishing deep with a sinking line, and it is effective in cold water or whenever the fish are less aggressive. In clear water and bright light, a speedier retrieve is usually the ticket. Try longer strips of 10 inches or more, with very brief pauses between them. This faster stripping motion is also a good bet when water temperatures are in the fish's comfort zone and whenever fish are aggressively feeding during the day.

The two-handed strip is done differently. After the cast, the rod is positioned high under the casting arm. Place it right in your armpit, such that the grip is covered and secured by your upper arm, with the reel protruding slightly to your back. At this point, both hands are free. Angle the rod tip down toward the

The one-handed strip is known to nearly all saltwater anglers and is very useful.

The two-handed, or hand-over-hand, strip is very popular too and much better at driving the hook home.

water, and reach up with either hand to the first stripping guide. Grasp the line just prior to where it enters the guide, and pull down on the line. Your hand might move 14 to 18 inches, or even farther. As the first hand is making its descent, the opposite hand is rising up to the stripping guide, where it now grasps the line. As the first hand reaches the bottom of the pull, the other begins to take line.

As with the one-handed strip, you should do a couple of quick pulls in order to get tight to the fly. Once that happens, you can settle into a steady rhythm, smoothly alternating hands to give the fly a steady, continuous motion. This is often a deadly retrieve. If you want a stop-and-go retrieve, it is a simple matter to insert pauses between pulls. Here, too, you should go slowly in cold or stained water or in low-light conditions. Moderate speeds are best in clear water during the daytime. High-speed retrieves occasionally work, especially on aggressive fish such as blues.

FEELING THE STRIKE AND SETTING THE HOOK

Some fish hit a fly so hard they practically pull the rod out of your hand. Even if you're daydreaming, you can't miss those strikes, and often the fish pretty much hook themselves. But in general, strikes are not that violent. And that means you have to be alert and on your toes.

I'm continually surprised to see how many anglers either miss strikes or fail to set the hook well. Fortunately, both problems are relatively easy to remedy. Missed strikes are nearly always because of inattention or slack in the line between angler and fly. For the inattentive angler, I recommend strong black coffee. Here's what to do to eliminate the slack: During the retrieve, the rod must be angled downward at roughly 45 degrees, so the tip is low to the water. Keep it there. Also keep the rod tip pointed at the fly; this is critical. It's easy to do in stillwater, but in a current, you'll have to slowly move the rod tip down-current in order to track the fly, while doing whatever is possible to remove the belly in the line.

Setting the hook requires a quick, firm motion and a sharp hook. When using the one-handed strip, I recommend what is called the slip strike. Immediately upon feeling a fish strike, drive the hook home with a single long strip. You'll instantly come tight to the fish. Do not raise the rod tip until the fish has turned and is taking line. With the two-handed strip, you do much the same thing. Upon sensing the strike, strip line quickly until you are firmly connected to the fish. Keep the rod tip down until the fish runs.

CHAPTER SIX

Canoes, Kayaks, and Rowboats

Saltwater fly rodders are increasingly using canoes, kayaks, and rowboats in pursuit of their sport. It's easy to understand why. Lightweight and relatively inexpensive, these hand-powered boats are also cheap to operate and maintain. They are nonpolluting, easy to transport, and can be launched practically anywhere. That's quite a lot in their favor, but there's more. These things are quiet, providing a great degree of stealth in shallow water, where many fly rodders like to operate. The ability to move in near silence while sitting so close to the water makes for an intimate angling adventure. You feel very much a part of the natural world. And when you cover stretches of water slowly, you tend to learn them in great detail. You will discover their fishing opportunities in a way that few other anglers ever will.

These boats do have their limitations, however. Let's establish some reasonable expectations. First off, it's a good idea to stay within a couple hundred yards of shore. A knowledgeable angler once told me he never paddles out farther than he would care to swim back, a point well taken. Safety considerations should always have the highest priority. Your range along the shore can be much greater. In fact, it's possible to travel a mile or more along the beach. These longer forays should be attempted only on calm days and where you're not forced to fight a current.

The use of a lightweight boat is also limited by weather and water conditions. A canoe or kayak is no place to be in a high wind, driving rain, or thunderstorm. A hand-powered craft is rarely a good choice in locations where swift currents prevail, nor is it a good idea in places where rough seas are the norm. Also avoid taking such a hand-powered craft into areas of heavy motorized boat traffic.

Top: *Lightweight boats are a great way to explore estuaries. Here an angler works the edges of a flat from my drift boat.* Bottom: *One of the most fun fish to catch in a lightweight boat is a little tunny, which can actually pull you around. I caught this one from my drift boat.*

Preparing for a day on the water. Note that the kayak is secured not only by straps over the hull, but also by ropes off the bow and stern.

Rowing or paddling requires strength and endurance, as well as skill. So even when weather and water conditions are ideal, you must factor in your personal qualifications. Too often I have seen people on the water who don't have the slightest clue how to properly use an oar or a paddle. Some of these people are further handicapped by paddles that are not of the proper size. Not only does the wrong paddle limit your range, but it could also spell trouble. Should the wind pick up without warning, you could suddenly find yourself unable to control your craft. So if you're new to the paddle sports, take a class in how to properly handle your craft, and consider a physical fitness program too.

Carrying capacity is another limitation. A lightweight craft can be expected to safely transport only so much. Therefore, it's essential that you know your craft's maximum capacity and that you never exceed it—even if it means leaving some tackle at home. You also must properly distribute the load. An unbalanced boat not only is difficult to propel and to keep on track, but also will tire even an experienced paddler. Worst of all, the craft will be highly unstable.

HULL DESIGN

I doubt you'll ever walk into a place offering a wide selection of rowboats, but you're likely to find a showroom full of canoes and kayaks. With so many to choose from, picking one can be a bit daunting. Naturally you'll want to get some professional advice, so look for a dealer that understands the needs of anglers. An outfitter that sells both boats and fly rods would be ideal. Here you can get the inside story on the latest hull designs from salespeople who regularly fly-fish from these boats. Such places do exist.

Canoe and kayak hulls come in a variety of lengths and widths. Longer hulls are faster, which is a good thing when you're chasing a school of fish. They also track better and are more likely to accommodate two people. On the other hand, longer hulls are less maneuverable and more awkward to carry, which is a major concern if you fish solo. Wider hulls are more stable, which is helpful when casting. Yet they are often slower and harder to paddle.

The sides and bottoms of canoes and kayaks come in a variety of shapes as well, each of which has its pluses and minuses. Some handle better in rough water, some track better in flat open water, some turn on a dime, some give you a drier ride, and so on. Thus every hull is designed around a series of compromises, and the real question is what combination of compromises is best for the fly-fishing you do. To simplify matters, canoe and kayak manufacturers usually list their models in categories according to the best uses. So you're apt to find models listed for touring, for river running, for whitewater, for general recreation, and for sportsmen. For fly fishing, the recreational or sporting types are usually the best. These hulls do not have the quick maneuverability that whitewater enthusiasts demand, nor are they as fast and efficient to paddle as a touring canoe. Instead, they have characteristics that make them well suited to anglers' needs. The hulls are stable at rest, which aids in casting; relatively easy to paddle; and good for occupants that need to move around.

PADDLES

Get expert advice on paddles as well. The right paddle will make your angling adventures easier and safer. Paddles come in different lengths and blade widths and are made from a variety of materials, including wood, aluminum, and graphite. A narrow-bladed paddle requires less effort to use and is the right choice for long-distance touring. Anglers often prefer, however, the power and steering control of a wider blade. The right paddle length depends on the shape of your boat and the length of your arms and torso. A wide kayak requires a longer paddle to operate than a narrow one. And the longer your arms, the longer the paddle you can comfortably use.

CANOES

Canoes have been around for a long time. Quiet and graceful looking, they are easy to paddle and very much at home in their surroundings. It's no wonder fly rodders have long been fascinated by them. Yes, some anglers consider them too tippy, but much depends on the experience of the crew. If you know what

This canoe is fully equipped with rod holders, special backrests, an anchoring system, and an electric trolling motor.

you're doing, canoes are quite capable craft. And so it is that today—thousands of years after the Native Americans first began plying the waterways of our continent in these sleek hulls— the canoe still exists and is available in more materials and designs than ever before.

Wooden canoes—be they wood and canvas or cedar strip—are gorgeous. At the same time, they tend to be expensive, harder to maintain, and often heavy, and for those reasons many anglers avoid them. Alternative hull materials include aluminum; composites such as carbon fiber, fiberglass, and Kevlar; and several types of plastics such as polyethylene and Royalex. Aluminum canoes are inexpensive and easy to take care of, but they are also noisy, and most anglers dislike that. The composites offer many advantages. They can be incredibly light, strong, and good looking and lend themselves to high-performance hull design. Some are expensive, however, and that pretty exterior tends to get banged up quickly. Plastic hulls are often a bit homely and heavy. On the other hand, they can be inexpensive, and the better ones are extremely rugged, ready to endure years of abuse.

The bow and stern of most canoes look much alike, but there is one type of canoe that is a notable exception. Some sporting models are made with a transom at one end so an outboard or electric motor can be mounted. These canoes— called square enders—do not have the flowing lines of a classic canoe, but they are exceedingly versatile. A special square-end canoe is currently built in Titusville, Florida. It's called the Gheenoe, after its creator, Harley Gheen. The Gheenoe is fairly large and very stable, enough so that two anglers can safely cast standing up and even walk around—which, by the way, is something I don't recommend in any other canoe. Given the size and shape of this hull, however, don't expect to paddle it. Rather, the Gheenoe is meant to be used with a motor or possibly poled.

Most canoes come with built-in flotation, but check to be sure that the one you're buying is no exception. I also recommend that you consider a brightly colored hull—yellow or red—as canoes sit fairly low in the water and power-boats may have a difficult time seeing you, particularly in a chop. It's up to you to do all you can to make your presence known.

KAYAKS

In the last ten years, recreational kayaking has taken the coast by storm. So great is their present popularity that kayaks are a common sight today along protected saltwater shorelines. Everywhere you turn, it seems you see one gliding by. In the salt, they outnumber canoes by a huge margin as the lightweight craft of choice.

Viewed from above, canoes are pretty much wide open from bow to stern, but that is not the case with a kayak. The topside of a kayak is an enclosed deck with one or more openings—called cockpits—in which the paddlers sit. The conventional kayak has a tight cockpit, one you have to almost shoehorn yourself into. A tight cockpit reduces the chance of water entering the hull, so it is preferable in rough conditions and for long-distance touring. If you capsize such a hull, you

right it by doing what is called an Eskimo roll. Anglers generally prefer kayaks with open cockpits, however, for several reasons. Open cockpits are much easier to get into and out of, and they allow you to store plenty of gear within arm's reach. If you capsize a kayak with an open cockpit, the Eskimo roll is useless. Once the boat inverts, it immediately fills with water. You must drop out of the hull, right the kayak, and then bail out the water. When the hull is fully afloat, you can attempt to climb back in, which, by the way, requires a special technique and is no small task.

Some kayaks come equipped with a rudder, a bladelike affair mounted

Open-cockpit kayaks are popular with many anglers.

off the stern, but unlike the rudder in most boats, this one has no tiller. Instead, you control this rudder's position by using foot pedals inside the hull. A rudder is likely going to add $100 or more to the cost of a kayak. Still, I think it's well worth it. For one thing, whether you're paddling at a snail's pace or at full bore in pursuit of a school of breaking fish, you can make instant course corrections without changing your cadence. That makes life easier, especially with hulls that are hard to turn—those 14 feet and longer.

Here's another advantage to a rudder, one that relates specifically to angling. There are going to be plenty of times when you have both hands busy casting or fighting a fish. And at that same moment, your kayak may be moving. It could be that the wind and current are shoving you along, or perhaps your rod is doubled over and a fish is towing you. If there are obstacles about, or if waves are coming at you, you'll need to steer. You could put the rod down and paddle, but that may be inconvenient, to say the least. A rudder might allow you to continue fishing and avoid trouble with a push of a pedal. In such cases, a rudder is a valuable friend.

Another style of kayak is the sit-on-top. Rather than slide into a cockpit, on these models you sit on what amounts to a recessed deck. That means you're higher off the water than in a conventional kayak, and that should make it easier to cast. Furthermore, sitting above the water permits air to circulate around you, and that helps you stay cooler in warm climates; where the water is cold, staying up can help keep you warmer. But as always, there is a price to pay for these advantages. Sitting above the waterline means that you are not as stable as with a traditional kayak. And the lack of a cockpit translates into less room for an angler to conveniently store fishing gear.

Whatever style of kayak you buy, check to see that it has adequate flotation. Airtight bulkheads are one solution and are often found in the touring models. Recreational models may have bulkheads too, but some rely on air bags or foam. If you own a kayak that does not have flotation, you should add some. Air bags are easy to install, or you can purchase solid blocks of foam at marine stores and cut them to fit. Flotation foam is also available as a two-part liquid that can be poured into place. It fills voids beautifully.

Kayaks sit even lower in the water than canoes, and as a result, they are at times almost invisible to powerboaters. This is a cause for real concern, and for that reason you should buy a kayak in a bright color—yellow or red—and avoid hulls in green or blue. When you choose your paddles, opt for a set with yellow blades. As you paddle, the blade comes momentarily overhead, helping to signal your position to other boaters. Even with a brightly colored hull and paddles, you need to do more. Consider mounting a flag on the rear of the kayak.

Bicycle shops sell one that works fine. It will make you much easier to spot from a distance.

Many kayakers complain of lower back pain. In some cases, this is a physical fitness issue, but the seats in many kayaks lack proper back support. Carefully examine the seats in any kayak you intend to buy. Sit in it at the store. See how comfortable the seat is and how well it braces your back. This seemingly small point could greatly affect how long you're able to fish. If you want to see a good seat design, check out the Phase-Three seats available in Wilderness System Kayaks.

Two unique kayak designs are available. One provides greatly enhanced stability, and the other provides high portability and ease of storage. The first, the Tribalance kayak, is designed to allow anglers to stand. To provide the necessary stability to the hull, the Tribalance sports outriggers mounted near the stern. I have not used this kayak, but the basic concept appears sound, although the outriggers likely come at a cost in terms of speed and maneuverability.

The second type, made by the Klepper Company of Germany, is a line of folding kayaks that has been around for many years. They are attractive, high-quality, tried-and-true craft. Unlike most recreational kayaks today, these boats are constructed as the Eskimos first did it, with an outer skin stretched over a rigid internal frame. But in this case, the outer skin is high-tech, and the rigid frame can be quickly disassembled. When it comes time to store the boat, you collapse the frame and remove it from the outer skin, and it all folds up into a neat package. It makes storage a breeze, and it gives you several options for transporting the boat. You can carry it on your back in a special duffle bag, and this is one kayak you can take along on an airplane.

ROWBOATS

Rowboats have a long and honorable history in saltwater angling. Two of the most famous big-game anglers of last century, Kip Farrington and Michael Lerner, used rowing dories to great advantage. In Nova Scotia, Farrington fought giant tuna from a 16-foot rowing dory. And Lerner even caught a 601-pound swordfish from a dory. Granted, the days of allowing huge beasts to tow us around are long gone. But it reminds us that rowing dories are durable and seaworthy angling craft.

I own and enjoy canoes and kayaks, but above all I like to row, so I'm a big fan of rowboats. But before I sing their praises, let me give you the minus side right up front. With the possible exception of a small dinghy, rowboats are typically heavier, harder to transport, harder to launch, and slower than either a canoe or a kayak. Moreover, rowing can be more physically demanding than paddling.

A drift boat may seem an unlikely candidate for estuaries, but they can work very well.

On the plus side, some dinghies have wide, flat bottoms that permit you to safely stand and cast, even in a slight chop. One such dinghy is a pram. A pram is a small portable rowboat with a flat bottom, a flat transom, and a blunt bow much like a barge or johnboat. The blunt bow may make for a wet ride in a chop, but prams carry a large load for their size and make excellent casting platforms. Not every dinghy is a pram, however. Some dinghies have pointed bows and V-type bottoms. These hulls move more easily in rough water than a pram, but they are less stable at rest and therefore harder to fly-fish from.

The freedom afforded by a flat-bottom boat is a godsend. Since you can stand up, you are no longer cramped in one position for long periods of time, as is the case with canoes and kayaks. From a standing position, you can spot structure better and spot fish quicker and from a much greater distance. On a flat bottom, it's also easier to cast standing up; you can cast farther; and it's possible to fire a cast in almost any direction. So if the fish suddenly erupt behind you, you can turn instantly and fire a fly there. Try that in a canoe or kayak. To top it off, I find it much easier to fight a fish, especially a big one, from an upright position.

Rowboats are also beamier than either a canoe or a kayak, and that means you have more room to perform basic angling operations, such as repairing a leader, changing spools, or finding and slipping on your rain jacket. Plus that beam translates into carrying capacity, so you can take along all the gear you want—spare rods, camera cases, coolers—and even a friend. And most rowboats have transoms ready and able to support a motor, should you decide to use one. All this adds up to why I find rowboats so desirable.

If you're looking for a pram, Spring Creek Prams (springcreekprams.com) is the largest manufacturer of custom-built fly-fishing prams. Many of their fine little craft are used for stillwater trout fishing, but estuary anglers on the West Coast use them for a wide range of salty species. These prams come in 8- or 10-foot lengths and can be ordered in wood, fiberglass, aluminum, or Kevlar. Another maker of quality custom prams is Greg Tatman (gregboats.com), who builds beautiful prams and rowboats and offers kits too.

I'm now rowing into my seventh season in a Hyde drift boat. Drift boats are intended for rivers, but I find them to be capable craft in the salt as well. They are easy to row over calm water, are rugged, attractive, and extremely stable. Their flared sides keep the hull extremely dry, and because they draw only inches of water, you can row up onto a flat. In addition, drift boats are totally designed with fly fishing in mind, with casting braces, comfortable seats, cup holders, hull anchoring systems, and plenty of storage. And they can accept a motor too.

On the downside, drift boats are more expensive than basic rowboats. They do not come with flotation, so you must add it. But the largest issue is this: Their hulls have considerable rocker to aid in maneuverability, but this also means that the boat can be quickly caught by the wind and pushed off track. And when the wind is pushing you off course, the rowing becomes harder. So I limit my rowing to days when the wind is 15 knots or less. Perhaps someday there will be a drift boat built specifically for the salt. Let's hope so.

A foldable rowboat is available from a company called Porta-Bote. Like the Klepper folding kayaks, this boat is a proven design that has been on the market worldwide for many years, and it's a snap to transport. The hull is advertised to be highly stable, fast, and extremely tough, and the Porta-Bote can be equipped with an electric or gasoline motor.

ORGANIZING YOUR FISHING TACKLE

Given the size of these boats, particularly canoes and kayaks, you're going to have to organize your tackle. You want things to be within easy reach, especially since fish make a habit of showing up unexpectedly. Yet at the same time, you do not want your gear to interfere in any way with the safe operation of the boat.

The biggest object to contend with, at least in terms of length, is your assembled fly rod. Rod holders are one solution; in fact, if you're using a kayak with a tight cockpit, it's probably your only option. Choose a rod holder that is adjustable, specifically designed to hold a fly rod, and impervious to salt. Mounting one is easy, although any hardware you use has to be stainless steel. In a canoe, the thwarts that brace the hull make a convenient place for a rod holder. On a kayak, you'll likely want to attach it to the deck.

Before you actually bolt down your rod holder, give its exact position some serious thought. You want the rod to be within easy reach, but you can't have it in a location that will hinder your ability to row or paddle. Also consider setting up your rod holder in a way that allows you to effectively troll a fly behind the boat.

Rod holders are not mandatory. In a kayak with an open cockpit, you can simply run the rod butt forward between your legs and have the rod tip on the gunwale pointing rearward. I do it and it works fine. In a canoe or rowboat, you can do much the same. Place the rod in the bottom of the boat, with the rod tip pointing toward the stern. Temporarily secure the rod somehow, or the strike of a strong fish could yank the rod overboard.

For your tackle, soft tackle bags make a lot of sense. They store compactly by conforming to the shape of the hull, and they rarely slide around as do hard-sided tackle boxes. When picking a soft tackle bag, look for one that is ready for the brine—no metal snaps or metal zipper parts, which will quickly corrode. Since these boats tend to get a bit wet inside, look for a waterproof bag or one that has at least a waterproof bottom. I like to pack the bottom of the bag with a large piece of foam, so that if the bag ever went overboard, it would float.

CASTING FROM A BOAT

In order to cast from a boat, you must have a considerable amount of loose line ready to shoot. If you allow that loose line to lie in the bottom of the boat, it may snag on everything in sight, so it pays to keep the bottom of your craft clean and free of obstacles. An alternative is to use a stripping basket—an invaluable tool when you need to get off a quick, clean cast. In a rowboat, you can stand up and strap the basket around your waist in the usual fashion. In a canoe or kayak, place the basket on the floor and strip line into it.

After you stop paddling, a canoe or kayak will continue to glide a considerable distance. In general, that's helpful, but not when you're bearing down on busting fish. When you're within range and you drop the paddle and fire a cast straight ahead into the school, the boat may continue forward toward the fly faster than you can retrieve line. This prevents you from getting tight to the fly; the fly gets no action; you get no hookup. Frustrating. Here's a solution: Before dropping the paddle, use it to change the boat's course slightly, turning it a bit broadside to the fish. Now when you cast, it's easy to properly retrieve the fly and set the hook.

TROLLING

Many anglers troll from these lightweight craft, although they may hate to admit it. Trolling is a deadly tactic. Over the course of the season, trolling a fly behind your boat can account for dozens of extra hookups you would not have gotten otherwise. But if you're going to do it, do it smartly. Allow the fly to travel well back from the boat, at least 60 feet. Make sure the drag is properly set and the rod is angled back toward the fly. These two things help assure a solid hook set. Whether you're using a rod holder or simply laying the rod in the boat, be sure that it is secure so that a fish will not pull it overboard. Check the fly occasionally to see that it is tracking straight and that it isn't fouled with seaweed or eelgrass.

The speed at which you troll is important. You must move the fly fast enough to impart action, but not so fast that fish are reluctant to give chase. Actually, the pace at which kayakers travel when cruising leisurely is an excellent speed for trolling. But you may have to vary your speed in order to be successful, and what works one day may not work the next. In clear water and bright light, a faster speed may be required. In cold water, stained water, or low light, a slower speed is probably best.

The depth at which the fly rides while trolling is another key consideration. If you're using a floating fly line, the fly is apt to wake right along the top. This can be effective, especially in water depths of less than 10 feet. In general, however, it's better to get the fly down a bit. Because the fly tends ride up in the water column as you troll, that's not so easy. Sinking lines and weighted flies will certainly help, and you may want to allow the line and fly plenty of time to descend before you start paddling.

Don't troll aimlessly. Focus on areas that have structure, current, or bait. An old trick that works well is to travel along the edge of a structure such as a bar or the drop-off at the edge of a flat. Many anglers troll by paddling or rowing in a straight line, but it is typically better to lazily zigzag along the structure. By zigzagging, you give the fly more action and cover more water. It works. And if you troll through a promising piece of water without a strike, circle back and troll through again using a different fly and perhaps even a different fly line.

BOATING COURTESY

Anglers in paddle craft regularly complain about discourteous powerboaters. And these complaints are often well founded. But by the same token, anglers in canoes and kayaks must recognize that they too need to respect the rights of others. When fishing near other boats, stay well out of casting range. Likewise, never fish so close to another boat that a hooked fish might result in tangled lines.

Give anglers on foot a wide berth too. Don't crowd their fishing to improve your own. If the situation demands that you travel within short range of these comrades, make as little commotion as possible. In some cases, you can take your paddles from the water and let the current or wind push you past. When passing near wading anglers, consider going behind them if it can be done safely, and announce your intention if you do so.

Lastly, boating courtesy doesn't end at the water's edge. Never allow your canoe or kayak to block a busy public boat ramp. Pull your craft to the side, or better yet, carry it up the ramp and leave it on the grass while you get the car. And if you see another boater struggling, offer to help. Some day you may need a favor in return.

BOATING SAFETY

Always have the proper safety equipment aboard. First and foremost, that means a personal flotation device (PFD) for every person aboard. No exceptions. Today PFDs are available in a wide variety of styles and colors to suit all tastes and types of recreation. In fact, there are so many PFDs on the market that choosing the right one can be a bit confusing.

If your boating takes you into fairly remote areas where rescue may take some time, or if you plan on traveling through very rough water, you need the best type of device available, a Type I offshore jacket. Most users of light paddle and oar craft do not fall into that category, however, and for them, the Type II near-shore buoyancy vest is usually sufficient. These are intended for areas where rescue would likely happen quickly.

Most PFDs gets their buoyancy from foam. Foam works well, but it also makes a PFD rather bulky, restricting mobility, and it can be hot when worn in the summer. Given all that, many boaters find them so inconvenient that they never wear them. Recognizing that problem, several years ago the Coast Guard approved inflatable PFDs. These devices look like a pair of wide suspenders. They are lightweight, permit freedom of movement, and are cooler than a conventional PFD. The inflatable PFDs come in two styles: those that self-inflate when they come into contact with water, and those that inflate when the wearer pulls a ripcord. Should either of these inflation methods fail, the user can also inflate the vest by forcing air through a tube. Some feel that inflatable PFDs are not the right choice for kayaks and canoes—that because these craft can so quickly capsize, conventional PFDs are safer. Still, an inflatable PFD that you are willing to wear beats a foam PFD that you aren't.

Personal flotation devices (PFDs) are a must. On the left is an inflatable PFD, and on the right is a conventional foam vest.

It's a good idea to take along a cell phone or a portable marine radio. You need to know the effective ranges of these devices, especially important with the cell phone. You don't want to find out in an emergency that you're outside the area of coverage. Marine radios come in waterproof models, but the cell phone should be carried in a small waterproof box, which can be found at a dive shop. With either, be sure that batteries are new.

Every boat needs a compass. Many people do not follow this simple advice; that's foolish. For one thing, on some parts of the coast, fog is an issue. It can overtake you suddenly and just as quickly obscure the way home. If room allows, along with your compass, you may want a small GPS unit as well. The price of these units has fallen considerably, and they have many uses both on and off the water. If you elect to carry one, carry spare batteries for it too.

If you plan to use a kayak with an open cockpit in rough water, consider getting a spray skirt, a cockpit cover with an opening for the paddler. Skirts are available in sizes to fit specific kayaks and come in both lightweight fabrics and heavier materials such as neoprene. Once in place, the skirt reduces the amount of water you take on from spray and wave. And a spray skirt can provide additional warmth in the cooler months.

An anchor is helpful too. It needn't be very big; a five-pound one should hold a kayak in calm water. Since you will not be in extremely deep water, you don't need a mountain of rope. A strong fish can actually tow a kayak or canoe a fair distance, what some call a Nantucket sleigh ride. In most situations, this can be fun, but in rough weather or wherever obstacles exist, being towed around could lead to trouble. For that reason, you may want to drop an anchor once you hook up. Here is another consideration: When you're being towed, it's very difficult to apply any real pressure to the fish. So dropping an anchor can be the only way to successfully fight a really big fish.

You should also have a sharp knife capable of slicing your anchor rope in an emergency. Because of the corrosive nature of salt water, you are best off with a stainless steel blade. Folding knives are very handy and come in many models. Some have multiple blades and an assortment of tools attached. I find these things to be a waste of time and would much rather have a single large blade, at least 3 inches in length, with enough backbone to take some abuse. Whatever knife you choose, keep it sharp and rust-free.

Inevitably you'll get some water in the boat, so you'll need something to remove it. A bilge scoop or sponge will take care of most problems, but if you have room aboard, a hand-operated bilge pump gives you added insurance.

Some type of signaling device is also important. An inexpensive whistle can be worn around your neck on a lanyard. An air horn—the kind that operates from a can of compressed air—is even better. It is relatively inexpensive, not terribly big, and extremely loud. If you need to get the attention of a powerboat bearing down on you, it should do the job.

For low-light fishing, navigation lights are required. Clamp-on battery-operated ones are available, and there are some portable high-power spotlights on the market at very reasonable prices. At the very least, you should have a waterproof flashlight aboard and spare batteries for it. Reflective tape or reflectors mounted on the hull are a good idea, especially if your hull is dark-colored.

Safety also means understanding the potential hazards you might encounter on the water and how to safely avoid them. Study navigation charts before you head out. Know your waters.

It's inevitable that at some point a powerboat is going to roar by you at high speed, and you're going to have to ride out the wake. Spend a little time practicing how to handle a wake, or a wave for that matter. You never want to get hit broadside, as this could cause your boat to capsize. As the wake approaches, point your boat at a slight angle into the waves. Stay cool, and paddle slowly toward the wake. Unless the wake is huge, you should be able to ride up over it.

On the water, stay alert for changes in the weather. An ominous dark cloud on the horizon may signal the approach of a thunderstorm. A shift in the wind may also be a concern, especially if the wind will now be going against the tide. The ride home could quickly get difficult.

Anchoring a small boat, especially when in a current, can be risky business, and some experienced boaters never anchor a canoe or kayak. Never simply lower the anchor over amidships and then tie it off to the gunwale. When the anchor grabs hold, the boat may swing broadside to the current and then suddenly lurch toward the water. This can be dangerous. It's far safer to anchor off the bow or stern. With most craft, there is more freeboard at the bow, and that is where the anchor should be tied off.

ROOFTOP CARRIERS

A canoe, kayak, or small rowboat can be easily transported in the back of a pickup truck, and a big station wagon may allow you to carry the boat with only a small portion hanging out the back. But with other types of vehicles, these craft are usually transported on the roof. The roof racks that come as standard equipment on most station wagons, vans, and SUVs are not very good. The crossbars often can't support a real load and tend to bend under the weight. Consider getting a professional-grade roof-rack system such as the ones manufactured by Thule and Yakima. They are not cheap, but good things rarely are. If you have trouble justifying the cost, think about this: These racks are great for many other uses. They can hold rod racks, storage boxes, bicycles, and other items.

Even with a good roof rack, you still have to secure the boat properly. Never use bungee cords to tie the hull to the rack; one good bump and the boat may come loose. If you use rope on the rack, be sure it is of good quality—no twine or clothesline—and tie good knots. Straps are really the answer. They provide a wider grip than rope, and because of it, they hold far better. Straps for canoes and kayaks are widely available and come with convenient locking clamps. Once the hull is tight to the rack, attach lines from the bow and stern to the bumper so the boat is secure enough even for highway speeds.

Canoes and dinghies are invariably carried upside down, and that is an excellent way to carry a kayak as well. Alternatively, some roof racks are designed to carry a kayak either right side up or on its side. If you elect to transport a kayak with its cockpit facing skyward, be especially careful. Under no circumstances can you allow the kayak to fill with rain. It not only would pose a serious problem for the hull and the roof rack, but it's downright dangerous as well. A rack designed to carry kayaks on their side has the advantage of allowing you to carry two or more kayaks on the same vehicle. This is a good system, but it has one downside: You must be strong enough and tall enough to lift a kayak up into the cradles.

Index

Bluefish, 2, 13, 16, 65, 67, 74, 75, 83,
    84, 112, 118, 126
  bite tippet for, 112
  poppers and, 75, 118
Boats, 19, 43, 50, 98, 127–142
  boat traffic, 19, 40, 43, 44, 127
  boating courtesy, 138, 139
  canoes, 43, 44, 57, 80, 85, 127, 130,
    131, 132
  casting from, 137
  kayaks, 43, 44, 57, 80, 85, 129, 132,
    133, 134
  rowboats, 43, 44, 57, 80, 85, 134,
    135, 136
  safety in, 43, 57, 97, 127, 129, 133,
    134, 139–142
  transporting, 142
  trolling, 138
Bonito. *See* Atlantic bonito
Bridges, 95, 98, 99
Bug repellent, 121
Bunker. *See* Atlantic menhaden

C
Calm conditions, 18, 49
Canoes, 43, 44, 127, 131, 132
Channels, fish in, 25, 38, 42, 44, 70, 95, 98
Chatham Inlet (Massachusetts), 23, 34
Cinder worms. *See* worm hatches
Circle hooks, 117
Clamworms. *See* worm hatches
Cleats, 32, 119
Clinch knot, 112
Coastal rivers, 78, 83, 84, 85, 94–98
  bends, 95
  bridges, 95, 98, 99
  dams, 95, 97, 98
  channels in, 95, 98
  currents in, 84, 85, 94, 98
  fish movements in, 83, 94, 95, 96
  islands, 95, 97

  riffles, 96, 97
  salinity in, 83
  tides in, 83, 84, 85, 93, 94, 95, 97
  tributaries in, 95, 96, 97
Cold fronts, 17. *See also* weather
Conditions, changing, 1–19. *See also*
    boat traffic, current, forage, light
    level, salinity, tides, time of current,
    water clarity, water temperature,
    weather patterns
Connetquot River State Park (New
    York), xi
Connecticut River, 14, 84, 85, 94, 95, 96
Coves. *See* bays and coves
Crabs, 68, 79
Creeks. *See* tidal creeks
Currents, effects of, 3, 4, 15, 24, 25, 33, 35,
    37, 57, 58, 59, 61 , 62, 63, 66, 67, 68,
    70, 71, 83, 84, 85, 94, 96, 97, 98, 110
  time of current, 7, 8, 24, 85

D
Dams, 95, 97, 98
Dawn. *See* dusk and dawn fishing
Dead-drift, 29, 88, 89, 90, 93
Deceiver. *See* Lefty's Deceiver
DEET, 121
Delta, 77
Diadromous, 16, 84
Drift boats, 135, 136
Drop-offs, 34, 58, 62, 77, 97, 98
Duck hunters, 19
Dusk and dawn fishing, 8, 74, 95

E
Eastern equine encephalitis, 121
Eel. *See* American eel
Eelgrass, 38, 46, 48, 58, 73
Estuaries, x, xi
  defined, x
  species of fish found in, xi

Reels. *See* fly reels
Regulations. *See* fishing regulations
Retrieve styles, 122, 123, 124, 125, 126
Rips, 25, 34, 41, 42, 57, 66, 68, 72
Riffle, 96
Rivers. *See* coastal rivers
River herring, 11, 75, 81, 83, 88, 96
Rods. *See* fly rods
Rowboats, 42, 44, 134, 135, 136
Rules. *See* General fishing rules

S

Safety, 19, 26, 32, 33, 34, 35, 38, 42, 43, 57,
   75, 76, 80, 97, 98, 127
Sandbars, 33, 34, 38, 57, 58, 68, 77
   in inlets, 33, 34, 38
   islands with, 57, 58, 97
Salinity, 15, 16, 62, 83
Saltwater cordgrass. *See* Spartina grass
Salt marshes, 78, 79, 85
Salt ponds and lagoons, 20–59
   defined, 20
   channels in, 20
   flats in, 40, 41, 44, 45, 46, 47, 48, 49, 50,
      51, 52
   inlets to, 20, 21, 22, 23, 24, 25, 26, 74
   islands in, 20, 38, 56, 57, 58
   jetties and. *See* jetties
   shoreline structures, 37, 58, 59
   sight fishing in, 20
   tidal creek in, 20
   worm hatches in, 91, 92
Saltwater wedge, 83, 84
Sand eels, 11, 46, 47, 50, 75, 88
Scorton Creek (Massachusetts), xi
Sea herring. *See* Atlantic sea herring
Sea-run trout, xi, xii, 2, 84, 87, 88
Seam, 25, 27, 29
Setting the hook, 126
Shad. *See* American shad,
   hickory shad

Shellfish bars. *See* oyster bars, and
   mussel bars
Shock tippet. *See* bite tippet
Shorelines, 38, 57, 58, 62, 63, 64, 69
Shrimp, 46, 64, 79
Sight fishing, 8, 14, 18, 19, 20, 49, 50, 51,
   52, 53, 54, 55, 58, 59, 101, 102
   casting techniques for, 52, 54, 55
   flies for, 53, 55
   fly rods for, 101, 102, 103
   making a "mud," 56
   methods of, 50, 51, 54, 55
   presenting a fly, 53, 54, 55, 56, 101
   seeing fish, 49, 50, 51
   skills for, 50, 52
   tides for, 48, 52
Silversides. *See* Atlantic silversides
Sinking fly lines, use for, 25, 27, 28, 29, 35,
   49, 57, 86, 88, 95, 97, 110
Sliders, 108, 117, 118
Snowmelt, 14, 83
Spartina grass, 7, 79, 80, 87
Spotted seatrout, 2, 68
Spring Creek Prams, 136
Squeteague. *See* weakfish
Squid, 46, 64, 79
Strike indicator, 29, 88, 89, 90, 91
Striped bass, 2, 13, 40, 46, 51, 55, 59, 62,
   74, 76, 84, 85, 88, 95, 100, 118, 123
Stripping basket, 52, 120, 137
Sunscreen, 121
Surgeon's knot, 112
Surgeon's loop, 111
Surflon Micro Supreme wire, 112, 113

T

Taut-line jigging, 99, 100
Ticks, 121
Tidal creeks, 58, 59, 66, 73, 78, 79, 85,
   87, 88
   bends in, 86